THE DANISH ACADEMY
OF PEOPLE AND NATURE

The Twenty-First Century

NEW READING
of
NEW TESTAMENT

Nataliya V. Poullo

Trafford
PUBLISHING

2011

ISBN: 978-1-4269-5684-3 (sc)
ISBN: 978-1-4269-5685-0 (hc)
ISBN: 978-1-4269-5404-7 (e)

Library of Congress Control Number: 2011901653

Trafford rev. 04/28/2011

 www.trafford.com

North America & international
toll-free: 1 888 232 4444 (USA & Canada)
phone: 250 383 6864 ♦ fax: 812 355 4082

For my son and my ⊏ *mom* ⊐
*without whom this book
would have never been written*

This book comes as the result of the research, which I carried during many years searching for the answers to the questions I first asked being ten years old. For the years, I collected tiny bricks of information and finally managed to complete the puzzle.

I would like to thank my son, who was the reason for this book to be written, and my mom, *who inspired me and helped me with my work. I want to thank Professor of Theology Per Bilde, Denmark, who provided me with the last missing pieces of information, and Vitaliy Belikov, Russia, who helped me to publish the book.*

I want to express special thanks to the people of the BBC and National Geographic Channels, who during the years issued a number of historic, archaeological, and ethnographical programs presenting a huge amount of data, which helped me in my research. Unfortunately, I have not saved titles of the programmes and the names of their authors, to whom I, however, express my deep gratitude.

CONTENTS

INTRODUCTION

"...during the certain epochs, when solar activity increases significantly and suddenly, we note simultaneous rise of neuro-psychological excitability of large masses of humans, which appears in increasing number of mass movements, psychical and psychopathological epidemics."

Professor Alexandr L. Chizhevsky
"Sunspots and psychoses" (Geliopsychology), 1928

No matter if we are believers or not, we all know the name of Jesus Christ. It is hard to find another person in the whole history of our civilization having the same huge influence on it. Just think, every other event of the history we mark with its date and letters BC, AC, AD, or CE, which means correspondingly before Christ, *ante Christum (before Christ, Latin)*, Anno Domini *(Year of God, Latin)*, and Christian or Common Era.

Twice a year, millions of people all over the world celebrate events of Jesus Christ's life: His birth and His resurrection. These events, as well as His teaching, seem to be the turning point of our history, our culture, and our civilization regardless of whether people believe in the reality of the stories and truthfulness of the teaching or not. Thus it is clear that not only specialists but many other people as well are

1

interested in the events of the ancient history. However, what do we really know about what happened that time in Jerusalem?

Generally speaking, all our notions considering the events are primarily based on the stories presented in the four canonical gospels, namely, gospels of Matthew, Mark, Luke, and John. Those who were more interested in the history probably read some apocryphal scripts as well; there are quite a lot of them, you know. All the scripts partly compliment and partly contradict each other. The reason is clear: none of the scripts was written at the exact time of the events by eyewitnesses; alas, nobody could foresee the future. Actually, it is better to say that we *have not yet found* documents written by eyewitnesses at the exact time of the events considering the events, and we are not sure if these documents still exist, and if so, where to search for them.

Experts say that the first written document describing life of Jesus Christ, namely, the gospel of Matthew, was written in approximately 60 AD. Before that time, the story travelled from mouth to mouth and was told and retold many times. Most probably, he who was next to tell the story changed it a bit though never meant it. You see, it is extremely difficult to tell the story precisely the same way as it was when being heard. First, it is almost impossible to recollect the story word by word when telling it later; and second, it is next to impossible to resist the temptation to make the story just a little bit more colourful than it was when being heard. People like good stories, no matter what century they live in. We know the same things happening now; that is why, though being interested the stories presented in mass media or told by someone, we do not always believe them. More than that, an exciting story often provokes rumours, which exaggerate a lot. Then, all of a sudden, we get a version of the story that differs so much from the original one, that we can hardly recognise it. Thus, we may conclude: it is only natural there are so many versions of the story.

2000 years have passed. We know approximately the time, the place, the main acting characters, and the general features of the events. No one can be sure about what really happened there. As I said, either we choose to believe the stories or not, and it is a private decision made by every one of us.

As for me, I have my own opinion about the events. Here in this book, I present you my version of the story. The version is based on the analysis of ancient texts, on the results of researches made by specialists in ancient history, ethnographic, folklore, psychology, and others, on the achievements of contemporary science, including research of The Danish Academy of People and Nature[1], which President I'm honoured to be, and on my personal experience. I shall tell you what I think about the events and the acting characters and explain why I do so. You are free to accept my point of view and to share it with me, or to deny it. After all, as I said, it is mere a question of belief.

In my suppositions I proceed from the following:

1. There is nothing more permanent than human nature. That is why the plays and stories written long and very long time ago, as those by Homer, Aesop, Shakespeare, and many other poets, writers and playwrights, still remain interesting and understandable in spite of the centuries that passed since they were written.

2. It is necessary to keep to the ancient texts as to the main sources of the information.

3. It is necessary to take into consideration the specific features of the epoch, of the country, of the cultural

traditions of people living there, and of the society of the time of the events[2].

4. I have an experience of my own, which about I have already written [1].

And now, let us forget all the explanations we once got and begin from the very beginning.

Notes

1. Read about The DACPN at the end of the book.

2. It's also good to remember that the official church authorities of that time didn't accept Jesus and His doctrine, which was alternative that time, exactly the same way, as church authorities nowadays don't accept any alternative point of view coming now; and that there were crowds of believers shouting: *"Crucify Him!"*

1

Questions

When I read gospels, there had always been several things that puzzled me. The feeling I had because of that was as annoying as a toothache. For example, when we read about Jesus talking to His disciples and to people in general, we notice that He *always* talked the same way, namely, as a teacher talks to his pupils in the classroom – and *only* this way. That is strange and absolutely not normal.

I am a teacher, my mother was a teacher, and my grandfather was a teacher (professors of universities, actually). Thus I can assure you: it is *absolutely impossible* for a person to behave him- or herself and to talk to the others *always* as a teacher in the classroom. *Everybody* needs to feel him- /herself as an equal among equals; *everybody* needs to chat, to laugh, and to relieve the mind from time to time.

You see, *to teach* is a work; and this work is not among easy ones. Hence, the first questions come: *whom* did Jesus talk to like an equal, and *with whom* could He just chat and laugh?

A couple of classic questions: *what was* Jesus' life like during the first 33 years, and *what* made Him to begin preaching?

A couple of classic questions more: why, among all the women Jesus healed, there was only Mary Magdalene, who permanently stayed with Him? *Where from* did Jesus get His ideas and points of views?

Now, considering Judas' betrayal. As we all know, Jesus knew about Judas' coming betrayal. *Why* did He neither stop Judas Himself nor let any of the disciples stop him? To the point, *why* was Peter's threefold renunciation of Jesus *never* interpreted as a betrayal? As I said, let us forget all the previously done explanations.

Why did Jesus trust the common money box to Judas; and *what happened* to it after Judas committed suicide?

Why did Judas throw out the money paid for the betrayal of Jesus? According to gospel of Mathew[1] – and we all know the story – Judas betrayed Jesus searching for money. Shall we believe that he, all of a sudden, changed his mind so much as to throw it out? The money that presumably was the main reason for his actions? Shall we accept, that he changed his mind abruptly so much, as even committed suicide?.. No, it definitely makes no much sense. So, what was *the real motive* of Judas' actions?

Then – Judas' kiss. Such nonsense! Why – *a kiss*? I would never believe that *a kiss* was a common way of greetings between men that time. On the contrary; homosexuality was a well-known phenomenon and it had already been condemned as a sin: the history of Sodom and Gomorrah had already been written[2]. It was possible to point to Jesus any other way, thus – *why was it a kiss*?

There was one more question, which always puzzled me: *why* did Mary Magdalene come to the tomb (sepulchre), where Jesus was buried, *"alone or with some women"*[3]. She would have known perfectly well that there was a sealed rock blocking the entrance of the tomb; she definitely knew she would need some help to move the rock aside, which was also mentioned in some scripts. However, according to the gospels, Mary came to the sepulchre all alone *or with some women.* Why did she act in such a strange or stupid way?

The gospels present this part of the story different ways, but all of them agrees in the following: *it was Mary Magdalene* to whom Angel gave the message of Jesus' resurrection, and *it was Mary Magdalene* to whom Jesus showed Himself the very first time after the resurrection. It confirms that at that very moment Mary Magdalene was all alone, no other women were present with her at the time. And now, there comes the next question: *why* did she leave the women and came to the sepulchre *alone,* if they went there *together?*

To the point, as we have already mentioned, the entrance to the sepulchre was blocked with the sealed rock. Why did the women, if there were several of them, go there *without men,* such as, e.g., members of their families, or friends, or the disciples? To unblock the sepulchre would be an impossible task even for *several* women. So, *what was the matter?*

And the last questions worth mentioning here are: where from did the idea about Jesus being the King come? As historians claim, that time there were lots of people preaching different types of new beliefs, but only Jesus was claimed to be a King of Jews; and why did people begin calling Him *Son of God?* Why He Himself called the God, "*My Father*"?

Notes:

1. 26:14-16; 47:48

2. Genesis 18:2; 19:4-5

3. Matthew 28:1; Mark 16:1-2; Luke 24:1; John 20:1

2

Jesus

We have agreed that the human nature – the way people feel and think – remains the same no matter what century people live in. If it was not like this, all that we call classic literature would have never existed as we would not be able to understand reasons of actions of the people living other time and other places, neither could we share their feelings. Happily enough, we all are the same: we smile when we are happy, and we grieve for our losses. We fell in love, and we hate; we work, we think about our problems and tasks, and try to find the solutions; we hope, and sometimes we become scared and desperate. That's why we perfectly well understand other people when reading about them in a book or watching plays and movies. The differences in cultures are not really thus important; they are tiny, we easily omit them. Hence, it would work perfectly well if we try to understand what happened then, 2000 years ago, examining the reasons and the feelings of the characters and relations existed among them, as if those people were our contemporaries and lived among us.

And now, let us try to find the right answers to the questions mentioned in the previous chapter as well as to some other questions that will appear later.

If we begin to think of Jesus Christ as of one of our contemporaries and consider that the ancient stories kept more or less to the facts, it becomes clear that Jesus was far from being an ordinarily person. It is obvious: His abilities greatly exceeded those of an average man.

The first thing worth mentioning here is that Jesus was a healer. Sure, His healing abilities did not appear suddenly, otherwise there should have been written something like, "…and all of a sudden He…" one or another place in the scripts. Instead we read that everybody accepted Jesus' actions of healing as something normal and quite predictable for Him – at least, His followers did. And so we admit: these actions were typical for Jesus making no wonder for those who accompanied Him permanently. Consequently, we may assume that His ability *to heal* appeared very early, long before He began preaching. Most probably, it appeared when Jesus still was a child.

I illustrate what I mean with the following examples. Imagine your little child came home crying loud because of the knee that was smashed and bleeding. Poor little one! Although there was not much you could do about it, you wanted to comfort the child and to quiet it. You began to blow on the bleeding knee and waved your hand over it – and all of a sudden, the knee stopped bleeding and the pain was gone. Or, suppose, you made coffee and spilled some of it onto yourself while pouring it in a cup. The pain was immense. Partly because of the pain, or, maybe, because you were just desperate, you waved your hand over the burned place and then, to your great surprise, you felt relief: your pain disappeared, and the skin came back to norm. Would you tell your friends and members of your family about it? Moreover, if once appeared, the ability *to heal* remained with you, thus you became able to help other people as well; would you tell about the *very first* time, when and how it all begun? I honestly do think so.

On the other hand, if your child being, let us say, five or six years old begins to perform such healings, I assure you: you would get used to it long before the child becomes a teenager. Just in a couple of years, you would accept such actions of his as normal and only possible.

To the point, the words of Mary, Jesus' mother, at the episode at the wedding, when she told Jesus to change water into wine (*John 2:1-9*), sounded exactly this habitual matter-of-fact way, "*Just do it!*" as we would say it today.

Some researchers claim Jesus to be an advanced doctor using herbs for medicinal purposes; I can easily believe it. More than that, I believe it would be only natural if so. Our contemporary reality demonstrates: no matter what a person did before he or she discovered the ability to heal in him-/herself, later on, they usually present themselves as healers. Often enough these people become interested in other forms of alternative medicine as well; they get special or additional education and further on continue to work in the branch of alternative medicine. If it happens nowadays, when we have advanced medical science using countless medications and sophisticated equipment, how could we possibly expect things to be different then, 2000 years ago, when the standards of living were unspeakably lower comparing to those of today, and when medical science itself was mostly a science of healing?

As a consequence we conclude: if a person those days showed ability to heal people, his way led him directly to medicine; almost certainly he would become a doctor.

Another ability of Jesus was clairvoyance talent. Actually, I do not think we should be much surprised about it. As people claim nowadays, the ability to heal often goes hand in hand with the clairvoyance talent[1]. It is actually quite an opposite thing that surprises me: there in the gospels, we can hardly find stories of Jesus predicting future for separate people, apart from very few episodes, which actually are the exceptions that confirm the rule.

Let us recollect, for example, the Last Supper. No, now, I do not mean the words Jesus said to Judas Iscariot. I mean the words He said to Peter. As you probably remember, Jesus said to Peter that that night, before the cock crowed, he would deny Jesus thrice (*Matthew 26:34*). The interesting thing though is that Jesus mentioned it *casually*, in a matter-of-fact tone, as something He did not specially think about. And the disciples accepted His prediction exactly the same way, i.e., as a natural and quite expected act of Jesus'. That proves: Jesus *had* the clairvoyance talent, *could* unmistakably predict the immediate future, and *did* it from time to time but… but He usually avoided doing it. In fact, it looks as if Jesus just did not want to show this talent of His. It is as well obvious that if the situation really was like described, there had to be a reason for Jesus to behave in this way.

To explain what I mean let us compare Jesus, for example, with Nostradamus.

Michel de Nostredame (1503 – 1566), usually Latinized to Nostradamus, was a French apothecary and reputed seer. He predicted much and made his fortune because of the talent of his. He published collections of prophecies, which made him famous worldwide.

Why did Jesus act differently? Why did He try to avoid making prophecies although He could not help doing it anyway? Why did He avoid telling people the future He saw for them? Has Jesus a special reason for hiding His clairvoyant talent? Or maybe, it was, rather, a habit?..

The answer is following: that time, as well as nowadays, as well as always, the one who began to tell *strange things* attracted special attention; and this attention was far from being friendly. As we see it now, in the most cases the person, telling *strange things*, provokes in surrounding him / her people feelings of dislike and perplexity mixed with thoughts of either stupidity or craziness / madness of the person. When those *strange things* go from the mouth of a child, it works even worse. In most cases, children reject those who are but a bit different from the majority of the group; they hardly accept the ones in their community, and very often they tease those merciless. The problem is well-known and gives many troubles nowadays. It is especially true, when the child shows the abilities known today as paranormal or supernatural.

It is obvious, Jesus' clairvoyance talent showed itself as early as His healing abilities, i.e., in His very childhood. Otherwise we could also expect to hear about the *first case* of His predictions. However, we know nothing either of His first healings or about the first predictions He made. They were not mentioned anywhere.

Thus it becomes clear, that all the years before the time, when all of a sudden Jesus began to preach the new belief, He lived without attracting *any* special attention; otherwise we knew much more about that period of His life, which we do not. That means: it all began when Jesus was but a boy. It was then, in His childhood, Jesus began to show His outrageous abilities, and at the same time He was taught the rules how to live in the society *without attracting any special attention.* Now, there comes another question: who taught Jesus these rules?

Without any hesitation we may answer: these people were Mary and Joseph, Jesus' parents and the only family He had. Who want a child to be safe and sound in the first place? Who are usually the persons most interested in wellbeing of a child? Of course, in the vast majority of cases these people are child's parents. I do not think Jesus' family was an exception. That is why I mean that there were Mary and Joseph who, in His very childhood, stopped Jesus from telling *all* the things He saw or could say. Obviously, they also taught Him *to think* before saying anything, which is a really tough thing to learn.

The reason for them to do so is obvious and was explained above: *they did not want Jesus to become called weird* and to be seized from the society and from other children. Neither did they want Him to attract the attention, which could be fatal for the child and for the whole family. Being neutral, Jesus would be accepted by neighbouring children, and the family could mix with the surrounding people.

It seems most probable, that at the same time, Jesus got advice from them to concentrate on the healing abilities He possessed, which He could use in future.

All this taken together gives us the reason why Jesus, although healing people, tried to hide His clairvoyance talent: it was just an old habit of His caused by the family's mode of living.

His faith, the faith of Jesus of Nazareth, was determined by His outrageous abilities and His parentage, of which we talk later.

Notes

1. It can be questioned, though, how high or how low the levels of these abilities are if any at all; and how many of those who claim to have the abilities possess them indeed.

3

Abilities

Talking about the abilities Jesus possessed, we can't help mentioning His ability to hypnotic suggestion. I am not the first to talk about it. The supposition, that Jesus possessed incredibly powerful abilities to hypnotic suggestion, was made long before me.

I myself suppose that Jesus possessed not only ability to hypnotic suggestion, but the ability to telepathy as well; i.e., he was able to "read" other people's minds.

Several places in the gospels we meet situations where Jesus answered the questions, which were *not pronounced*. The act obviously looks habitual making no wonder either for Him, or for those who accompanied Him permanently. When Jesus did it, His words sounded exactly the same casual matter-of-fact way as when He predicted the immediate future, which we talked about in the previous chapter; and that allows us to make the conclusion.

There is actually one more thing I would like to underline here: the cases, when Jesus answered unpronounced questions, occurred as spontaneous as appearance of His clairvoyance talent.

Out of my experience I must say that cases of both clairvoyance and mind reading, as a rule, occur spontaneously and sporadic. You never know when it happens, neither when it happens next time; thus you are never prepared for the situation. When it happens and you "read" another person's mind, you seem *to listen* to what the person says. You never suspect that the person does not *speak out and pronounce* the words, but *thinks* them. You listen to the words that sound distinct and loud, as if being pronounced near you; more than that, the whole thing sounds as being said *especially for you to answer*. That is the reason why you answer aloud: you just do not understand you are answering not the *words*, but the *thoughts* of another person.

Your close relatives and friends can get accustomed to this peculiarity of yours and forgive you for such actions. But if it happens somewhere else, people begin to glance at you out of the corners of their eyes in, let us say, *not quite friendly way*. Then, usually, they try to leave you as quick as possible; and if they are acquaintances of yours, they prefer to avoid you in the future. People never forgive those, who see them the way they really are, but not the way they want to be seen.

There is another aspect of the situation as well. As we know today, brain activity as well as activity of nervous system in general occurs due to electric impulses passing through it and biochemical reactions caused by the impulses. We know as well that electromagnetic radiation has a profound effect on all living organisms. No matter what century we live in, the invisible electromagnetic field of the Earth permeates the entire space and affects all the inhabitants thereof. The state of the electromagnetic field of the Earth depends, in its turn, on solar activity, which influences it greatly. Almost 100 years ago, an outstanding Russian scientist Professor A. L. Chizhevsky[1] proved connection existing between activity of the Sun and physiological and psychological reactions of human beings and all living on the Earth. Thus, we may conclude that the state, when *the strange things* like those above mentioned happen, is a phenomenon of the nervous system reaction caused by a certain kind of solar activity and perhaps some other geo-magnetic factors connected with it.

Could it be that under certain circumstances, brains of some people become able to "receive" and to "decode" signals produced by brains of other people, i.e., their thoughts? Is it possible, that these unique people have some tiny peculiarities in functioning of their brains, which makes the process of "receiving" and "decoding" of other people's minds signals available for them? How much do we really know about our "thinking" organ?

Sure, it happens very seldom, and of course, there are but a few people having such abilities. That is the reason why it is so difficult not only to register and study the phenomena, but even to believe its existence.

Still, many of us have at least once experienced *the strange state* usually called "the sixth sense". If you are one of those lucky who has experienced it, you have probably noticed, that the feeling comes unexpectedly, all of a sudden. Those who experienced the feeling several times could have noticed, that sometimes you are able to provoke it, but usually it comes unexpectedly. Moreover, if you want to arouse the feeling on purpose, you almost never succeed in it no matter how eager you are and how hard you try. Now, when we take into consideration all the above mentioned, meaning the solar activity and the geo-magnetic factors caused by it, we clearly understand, why these cases are so seldom and their appearance is so unpredictable.

As for the hypnotic suggestions performed by Jesus, I would say, that particularly I do not think Jesus Himself knew He hypnotized people. I think He honestly believed He transformed the reality. Our contemporary hypnotists can easily suggest to the audience or to a person that there is not water, but a good wine in the glass from which the person(s) drink(s). The result of the action of the liquid on the person will be matching – as long as the person stays under the suggestion. When the hypnotic suggestion is removed by the performer all the effects caused by the suggestion disappear without a trace.

And that is something Jesus never did: He never "unhypnotized" people. Why did He never do it? The explanation is simple: He just did not know He *had* hypnotized them. Actually, it seems as if Jesus simultaneously hypnotised Himself too; otherwise He would have known there was not wine but water in the jars. However, He never suspected it.

Jesus hypnotized people momentarily, without mesmerizing them – and we can see the similar actions performed by our contemporary hypnotists– and never suspected it Himself. He really believed He changed the reality; because what else is reality if not that we experience by our senses? The philosophers, who found out how much real is the reality reflected by our senses, lived another time, other places…

Here, I would like to quote a Bulgarian writer Pavel Vezhinov. "When a person dies, the whole world dies together with him… Everything we call "inner life of a person" is, in fact, something not quite real as the clouds reflected on the surface of a lake When the wind blows and there come ripples on the surface of the lake, the reflections disappear; but it does not mean that the real clouds disappear as well. Everything happened that moment on the surface of the lake is death without either meaning or importance". It sounds sad, but it is true.

Now, I illustrate what I mean by hypnotic actions of Jesus' words on people with a couple of examples.

Jesus saw Simon (Peter) and his brother Andrew casting a net into the sea. He said to them, *"Follow Me"*. They *straightaway* left their nets and followed Him. Later, Jesus saw two other brothers: James, the son of Zebedee, and John, his brother, in a boat with Zebedee, their father, mending their nets. He called them too, and they *immediately* left the boat and their father and followed Him (*Mathew 4:18-22*). In some time, Jesus saw a man named Matthew, sitting in the customhouse and said to him, *"Follow Me"*. And Matthew did exactly the same: he *immediately* rose and followed Jesus (*Mathew 9:9*).

We have to admit that such immediate obedience of adult people is rather odd. But it does not seem weird a bit, if we accept the supposition of the hypnotic suggestion preformed by Jesus. Our contemporary hypnotists demonstrate us exactly the same reactions of people to their words and actions.

Let's take another example confirming that there was hypnotic suggestion, which made people to react to the words of Jesus *"Follow Me"*. In the gospels, we read of countless people healed by Jesus. In spite of that, His disciples still had some doubts; there in the gospels we read several times that Jesus reproved them for their lack of faith in Him. The strange thing though is that *none of the disciples never ever thought of the possibility to leave Jesus and to return to their previous lives.* No matter whether they believed Jesus or doubted Him, agreed or disagreed with Him and His decisions, they continued to follow Him permanently. Even after Jesus' death, when they were completely at a loss and did not know what to do, the idea of taking home and returning to their previous lives and occupations never occurred to them.

The reason is clear – they were hypnotized by Jesus *to leave everything they did and to follow Him!* Every one of them received the order he had to obey, which they did ever since.

After Jesus' death, it became impossible for them to fulfil the order. That is why they were at a loss: *they were not able to follow the task they were given, which became the most important task of their lives.* At the same time they were not able to think about returning to their homes and to their previous lives. So, what did they have to do?

Then one of the disciples – particularly I think it was Peter – got an idea: it was possible to understand the words of Jesus *"Follow me"* not only literally, but also figuratively. In this way, they could continue to fulfil the mission of their lives, i.e., they became able to "follow Him" in the figurative way by continuing His work. The way out was found, the decision was made: they would *follow Him* by disseminating the new doctrine, His teaching. Then, the disciples left their native places. They went to different countries preaching Jesus' doctrine, no matter what price they had to pay for it. Poor them…

By the way, have you noticed that not every one of those who heard the words of Jesus *"Follow me"* obeyed Him at once or at all? Let us take, for example, Zebedee, the father of the above-mentioned brothers James and John, and the hired servants of his who were present there at the stage as well (*Mark 1:20*). For all those people the words of Jesus meant nothing.

Why? Could it be that these people did not obey Jesus just because He addressed His words *only* to the brothers[2]? Or did it happen, because that time the brothers were working together with their father and *were ready* to obey? Was Zebedee resistant against the influence of the words of Jesus, because being the head of his family and the head of the working team he himself was a leader at the moment of the speech; thus, Zebedee would rather *give* orders than *obey* them? As for the hired servants, perhaps, they had immune to any other influence but Zebedee's simply because they knew perfectly well who paid them and for what? If we look at the situation from this point of view, we easily notice: there were only the brothers who were "available" for the obedience of the external influence.

Actually, the explanations can be different. There was just one thing in this part of the story which I always wondered about: why Jesus said the words *"Follow me"* to these people in particular? Could it be, that these people became His disciples *only* because they responded the influence and obeyed Him? That is one of the questions that will never be answered...

Returning to our discussion of the abilities we should notice that if we cast a look at the history of mankind, it is possible to find several examples of people possessing outrageous abilities similar to those of Jesus. Though very seldom, such people appear from time to time in different countries. Let us take just one example. Not long time ago, there lived a man, who had an unbelievably strong power of hypnotic suggestion and was able to perform "mind-reading". The man's name was Wolf Messing.

Wolf Messing (1899-1974) was born in Gora Kalwaria, Poland, in a Jewish family. There were four brothers in the family, but Wolf was a special boy. Being only four years old, he could learn by heart whole pages of Talmud and suffered of sleep-disorder: he was a sleepwalker in correspondence to the phases of the Moon.

At the age of eleven, Wolf Messing run from the home of his parents. He took the first passenger train leaving the station of the little town where his family lived. The train was to Berlin, which became the first new city in the full of travelling life of Wolf Messing. There under the trip, his *special* abilities showed themselves at the very first time. That is how it happened.

Wolf Messing had almost no money with him; that's why he hadn't bought the ticket for the trip. Soon after, a train conductor came checking the tickets. Poor boy was horrified; he hid himself under the bench. He hoped the conductor would not notice him. But the hopes were in vain. The conductor looked at him and said, "Now, show me your ticket, boy!" Not knowing exactly what to do, Wolf Messing took a scrap of a newspaper from the floor and handed it to the conductor. He was looking directly into the conductor's eyes thinking in despair, "THAT'S THE TICKET! BELIEVE IT!" He put into the thought all the wishes, all the strength of his frightened soul. The conductor took the paper, hesitated a moment or two, and then he punched it and smiled, "Silly boy, why are you hiding yourself under the bench, if you have a valid ticket? Take your place ON the bench!" That was the beginning of the strange life of Wolf Messing.

There were bright and there were black pages in it. There in Berlin, he was dying of hunger. Due to a coincidence, he began to entertain at a circus, and then came the success. Before the World War 2, Wolf Messing visited several countries as an enigmatic "psychic entertainer". He became famous. During a performance in 1937 in Poland, he was asked a question about what would happen if Adolf Hitler invades Poland. Wolf Messing answered without hesitation, "If Hitler turns on East, Germany will fall." His words were reported to the heads of Wehrmacht, and the reward of 200.000 Reich Marks was offered for his head.

In 1939, the German troops occupied Poland. Soon, in one of the streets of Warsaw, Wolf Messing was recognized by Nazi patrol, arrested and taken into the custody. There he managed to gather in his cell all those who were on duty on the first floor, where the cell was, mesmerized them, left the cell, jumped out of an open window into the street, and got free. While landing, he damaged both his legs, but he escaped from the prison.

Then, he fled to the USSR. Stalin called for him, and Wolf Messing had to prove the abilities. While doing it, he made incredible things. For example, he had to walk into the Moscow Gosbank and to get a huge amount of money using just the power of his mind. He came back with 100.000 rubles. After showing the money to the inspecting agents, Messing together with the agents came to the bank again. When Messing returned to the bank counter and handed back the money, the cashier looked at the money in surprise, looked at Messing then at the blank sheet of paper. Then he fell to the floor with a heart attack. "Luckily, it wasn't fatal," wrote Messing later in his memories. He made amazing things, and he was a man of many puzzles.

Though Wolf Messing and his life story deserve special attention, this book is not about it. There is only one thing I want to underline here: there are people who possess *the special abilities,* and these people appear from time to time. Though it happens very seldom, and the specific features of their abilities vary a lot, these people still exist. During their lives, they perform strange things, which arises talks, questions, and doubts, and which are called miracles or lies[3] when told about later.

To the point, I do not think we should insist on keeping to the exact number of thousands of people mentioned in gospels. Historians give quite different figures considering population of the areas at the time of the events, and they long from being so much impressive. As we take the historic aspect, it is better to keep in mind these figures.

There was one more thing about Jesus Christ and Wolf Messing that they had in common. Both of them could perform incredible things, but… it was not always they could perform that. Sometimes, both of them could neither demonstrate, nor employ their outrageous abilities. For example, Jesus could do nothing in front of Herod (*Luke 23:8-9*). Wolf Messing was arrested twice, in Warsaw by Nazi and in the USSR by NKVD, but couldn't do anything about it. I doubt it was a question of principles for either of them. Besides, we have almost the same situation mentioned in the gospel,

> "And He did not many mighty works there, because of their unbelief," *(Matthew 13:58).*

The excuse is different, but situation is the same: Jesus did not succeed in performing the expected miracles.

It is possible to find other examples to prove the similarity between these two people. Sometimes they both performed astonishing things, miracles, but sometimes they were not able to do anything. Taking into consideration existence of the objective and subjective factors, such as solar and geo-magnetic activity and their influence on the people, which I told about in the beginning of the chapter, everything comes to their places. It was just too bad, that the factors worked sometimes wrong for both of them, for Wolf Messing and for Jesus Christ.

Notes

1. Professor Alexandr Leonidovich Chizhevsky (1897 – 1964), an outstanding Russian scientist, a founder of such sciences as cosmic biology, geliobiology, geliomedicin, geliopsychology, etc.

2. Which actually once again confirms the idea of the hypnotic suggestion performed by Jesus.

3. To the point, according to a study led by Florida State University, USA, Professor of Oceanography Doron Nof, it is more likely that Jesus walked on an isolated patch of floating ice.

   The study points to a rare combination of optimal water and atmospheric conditions for development of a unique localized freezing phenomenon, that Nof and his co-authors call "springs ice".

   In what is now northern Israel, such ice could have formed on the cold freshwater surface of the Sea of Galilee – known as Lake Kinneret by modern-day Israelis – when already chilly temperatures briefly plummeted during one of the two protracted cold periods between 2.500 and 1.500 years ago, [2].

4

Birth

Well, as we anyway have no other sources of information but gospels, let us fish the tiny pieces of truth out of what we have. Still, let us remember, that nowadays we know much more than people living 2.000 years ago. Thus, the information presented by the scripts can be compared to the news told by a child, which he saw on television the day before yesterday. With that I mean, that the information in its general features is more or less correct, but lacks a great number of facts, details, and logical connections between causes and effects.

Let us begin from the very beginning, i.e., from before the moment of Jesus' birth.

Now, what do we have here? Immaculate Conception, carpenter from Nazareth, gifts of the Wise Men, and the star of Bethlehem.

Let us take Immaculate Conception first. Is it possible? – NEVER. As I already said, I do not discuss questions of belief but keep to the reality

In general, as we know nowadays, the Immaculate Conception *is* possible. In fact, there are two possible ways of Immaculate Conception:

1. medical impregnation; and
2. chromosome duplication, which occurs with some protozoa and which, according to scientists, is theoretically possible for more complicated living forms including human beings.

Well, as for medical impregnation, we can exclude it at once. The procedure is difficult and does not always give the desirable result even nowadays. That leads us to the only possibility, i.e., to the chromosome duplication. Spontaneous chromosome duplication, of course. Let us say, it was the only one exceptional unique case of spontaneous chromosome duplication in the ovule of a human being in the whole history of humankind.

No, anyway, it does not work. In this case, Mary would have given birth to *a girl*, and this girl had to be identical to her mother having precisely the same setting of chromosomes. To accept the possibility of spontaneous chromosome duplication in the ovule of a human being with simultaneous falling out of some genes (perhaps as a result of a mutation), and not just "some" genes, but those responsible for the gender of the baby – don't you think it sounds too much unreal?

That leads us to the fact that Jesus Christ was born because of the normal procedure, i.e., as a result of a sexual intercourse that took place between a man and a woman; i.e., as all the children of the world.

As for the Immaculate Conception, I think the story was invented later. Actually, it is obvious that the story was of primary importance, and that caused its survival throughout the centuries.

Who invented the story, why, and for what purpose? Later, at the end of the chapter, we'll learn about it.

Right now, I would like to put the subject aside for a while and to say a couple of words about the two oldest Christian Churches; namely, about the Catholic Church and about the Orthodox Church.

Members of the Orthodox Church claim the Church to be the oldest one. According to them, the Church was established in 33 AD by Jesus Christ Himself among Greeks living in Jerusalem. It is commonly admitted, that of all the contemporary Christian Churches, the Orthodox Church keeps the general traits and characteristics of the early Christianity in the highest extent.

The time of the Roman-Catholic Church foundation is not thus clear. They say that the Christian Church in Rome first appeared approximately in 50 AD. Actually, taking into consideration the 2.000 years that passed since, the difference in some twenty years does not matter much.

The two Christian Churches were established almost at the same time, and existed side by side during the centuries having much in common. Nevertheless, there still are some differences and disagreements in their traditions and conceptions. Let us take, for example, the holiday of Immaculate Conception (December 8). The holiday exists in traditions of the Catholic Church[1], but not in the Orthodox Church's traditions.

The fact, that the holiday is not equally celebrated in both Christian traditions seems to me rather strange. You see, I would consider it to be only natural if the holiday equally existed in both traditions being established by Jesus Christ Himself – especially if He meant that the Immaculate Conception took place indeed having in mind any meaning of the word. But He never did it. Moreover, the oldest and the most "traditional" Orthodox Church *mentions* and respects the event, but does not *celebrate* it. This obviously indicates that the fact of Immaculate Conception was of much more importance to the Catholic than to the Orthodox Church.

Next. According to the Catholic tradition, the main and the most celebrated holiday of the year is Christmas. In the Orthodox Church, the most important and the most celebrated holiday of the year is Easter. It seems to me rather strange too. No, I do not question importance of both events. Every living person on the Earth was born and, according to the most cultural traditions, this event is to be celebrated. But you see, according to the tale, the *only one* rose from the death. That's why the event, no matter if it is only believed to happen or happened indeed, is worth greater celebration[2].

Here comes one more question: why did the birth of Jesus become the most important holiday of the year for the Catholic Church? Could it be that Jesus and His birth meant more to His Jewish pupils, than to the Greek ones? Is it possible, that the disciples, who were Jews by origin, knew or guessed something about Jesus, which was of primary importance to them, but meant nothing or almost nothing to the group of His Greek pupils, who laid the foundation of the church, which we now call Orthodox?

Questions… questions… and more questions.

I want to attract your attention to one more peculiarity of the story. There in the gospels, we read, that Jesus communicated with lots of people. Nevertheless, there were not so many *acting* characters of the story. First, they were Jesus Himself, Mary, His mother, Peter (Simon), Judas Iscariot, and Mary Magdalene also called Mary of Magdala. All the others, including Joseph – Mary's husband, and the rest of disciples, are no more than extras. The importance of the disciples becomes significant only after Jesus' death, as for Joseph – he is of no interest at all, and so are Jesus' brothers and sisters. Why were all these people so *unimportant* to the storytellers? Soon, we'll answer the question.

And now, I want us to return to the moment of Jesus' birth – but let us accept, that He was born as all the others on the Earth and had a mother *and* a father.

Gospel of Matthew (*1:1-17*) gives us the book of generation of Jesus Christ, the son of David, the son of Abraham. There is no need to quote it here and I am not going to do it. The most important thing is that the book of generation exists.

Now, let us recollect the fact, that gospel of Matthew is the earliest gospel dated approximately 60 AC. That means that in this particular case, there is a high probability of the existence of the genuine information considering the ancestors of Jesus Christ. Why? You see, because always, even now, children all over the world learn by heart origin of their kings, patriarchs, and rulers, and the order, in which they changed each other on the thrones.

With this I mean, I do believe that Jesus Christ was the descendant of legendary Jewish kings.

But I do not believe that Joseph, Mary's husband, was the descendant of the kings indeed. Too *unimportant* his role in the story was, if we take into consideration the way he was presented in the gospels. I would most likely accept that it was Mary, Jesus' mother, who was the real descendant of the royal bloodline.

By the way, that supposition was also made long before me. There was just one problem: the book of generation of Jesus Christ, given in gospel of Matthew, names not Mary, but Joseph. However, what if it was not true? What if that fact was forged by fault or in purpose?

Let's try to find the answer to the question.

That time, the origin and the inheritance of a person preceded only by male relatives of the family; which is still typical for many cultures and countries. But what would happen, if of the whole royal family, there was only one girl left alive?

In this case, first, she would need protection; second, she would attract attention to herself, no doubt about it. Not less attention would be paid to her child, if she got one. It is as well clear that she would never be allowed to stay alone.

Doesn't it resemble the situation we read about in gospels? The attention paid to Mary is incomparable to that paid to her husband, Joseph, in spite of the fact that the role of men in the society those days was much more important than that of women – with only one exception, namely, when we talk about a common man and a woman of royal origin.

More than that, in all the stories Joseph is rather, so to say, "isolated" from Mary and her son, Jesus, as if he who told the story wanted to underline: Joseph had nothing to do either with Mary, or with the son, Jesus.

Strictly speaking, Joseph plays in the story the role not of a husband, but of a person who protects, serves, and takes care of Mary, as if she really was a person of royal blood in exile, and he was a man authorized by the court to accompany her being responsible for her and her child's wellbeing.

Nevertheless, there in the gospels we read: Joseph was Mary's husband. So, what was there indeed?

I believe it was like that: the book of generation of Jesus presented by gospel of Matthew is genuine. Jesus *was* the direct descendant of legendary kings. Taking into consideration, that Jewish people brought their identity, language, culture, and knowledge of their history through the centuries no matter where and for how long time they stayed among other nations, I do not believe they could forget the descendants of their royal family. That is why they learned by heart the names of their kings… but the last ones – for the sake of their security, perhaps.

Yes, there were other kings and rulers, but the family of genuine kings meant much more in the minds of the people.

The supposition of purposeful falsification of Jesus' origin is circumstantially proved by the fact, that the history of King David's life was changed and rewritten several times correspondingly to the needs of the rulers, which historians claim undoubtedly.

The necessity of keeping in secret existence of the members of the royal family, their names, and the places of their living was obviously caused by the hard times in the history of Jewish people: Romans ruled the country, and power of pharaohs was not forgotten yet.

Could it be that there were some people or an organization responsible for hiding and protection of the members of the royal family, who served them and kept in secret places of their living? Who could be these people, if they existed? Could they be, perhaps, priests?

Actually, it is possible. And if so, these priests definitely did not belong to the ruling church. That time, as well as nowadays, there was more than one active church. If these people were representatives of one of them, keeping the knowledge of descendants of King David, they had to be representatives of the oldest one.

Common people knew nothing for sure about the royal family and its members. Still, the rumours of its existence, i.e., of existence of the descendants of the legendary kings circulated among people. As a result of the rumours, the Massacre of the Innocents took place: the rumours of the birth of the boy, who could possibly raise an insurrection making attempt to restore the throne and the kingdom, reached the highest levels of the society.

Here, we have one more indirect proof of the supposition, that Mary was the last person of the royal family alive: *a girl* was not dangerous to the authorities; a woman could not inherit either the throne, or the power. *She* was not a threat – but *a boy*, her son, could become one.

Now, let us suppose that Mary really was the only representative of the House of David alive – and the last one. There were no more direct descendants of the royal family. It is not known to us either she had any distant relatives, or maybe there were none. A young woman in the world of men? Alone?! A woman of such origin and such importance?!! Even now, such situation would cause troubles, but that time, the situation would be considered as absolutely inappropriate. The girl had to be protected, get married, and give birth to a child (preferable children) to ensure survival of the royal family.

History tells us not much about how Mary met Joseph. Maybe she knew him in advance, or got acquainted with him occasionally, or there was somebody (Angel[3], perhaps?) who pointed Joseph to her or her to Joseph. One thing is for sure: Mary and Joseph got married and, in spite of the typical leading role of men in families and the society, Josef always was subordinate to Mary. At least, that is how the situation is depicted in gospels.

Isn't it here we may find the explanation of the story of Immaculate Conception? The royal blood must not be mixed with the blood of common people[4], *mésalliance* is unacceptable. As we know, the tradition survived throughout the centuries and still exists some places. Besides, let us remember, we talk about the people, who rate their authenticity to the highest extent.

And if Mary indeed had royal origin, the coming of the Wise Men to the child's cradle was absolutely logical and normal. More than that, it was *necessary* as the Wise Men had to give the evidence of the birth of the heir. They should have seen the baby to proof its birth, the birth of a new king. The tradition exists even now: newborn babies of royal families are to be shown to public. Besides, we are all interested in the events happening in royal families, especially in the marriages and births; and not only in those taking place in families of people of royal or noble origin, but in lives of celebrities in general.

As for the Wise Men, perhaps, they had to fulfil another task as well: presumably, they had to make a description of the baby to insure they can recognise it later to exclude the substitution if any. Consequently, these three Wise Men should be some of the priests belonging to the special group that kept and protected the information about the royal family and its members.

It did not matter that the royal family lived in exile and any slip of the information about their existence was a threat to their lives. The most important thing was – THEY EXISTED; that gave Jewish people strength to survive and hope for the future. And so, the Wise Men left their places and came to give the evidence of the birth of the royal baby. The king was born; a new hope appeared for people of Israel.

By the way, I suppose that the place of birth *in stables* was not a coincidental one; obviously, it was carefully chosen. Most probably, it was done by the same men, who came later to testify the birth of the new king. These people had to select the place to guarantee safety and comfort of the mother and the baby to ensure their survival, and to provide their security, which first of all included preventing any undesirable attention that could be fatal to both of them.

The choice was made; the instructions were delivered to Joseph and Mary. The coullpe left their home and moved to the pointed place. That is why the Wise Men knew exactly where to go to see the newborn Jesus.

To the point, have you ever tried to choose a star in the sky and to find the exact place to stand precisely under it? I have. If you haven't – try then; you'll see what I mean. There is no way you find the star in the sky and later on find the exact place on the ground to stand precisely under it. Thus, the tale:

> "When they heard the king, they departed; and behold, the star which they had seen in the East went before them, till it came and stood over where the young Child was." *(Mathew, 2:9)*

is an absolute fiction.

The situation with Mary giving birth to Jesus was rather peculiar and complicated indeed. A giving birth woman always attracts attention, which was very dangerous for them all. Besides, there was necessary to foresee the possibility for strangers to come to look at the newborn child and to testify its birth; and that again should not attract any attention. That was the task to be fulfilled.

In other words, when a woman gave birth to a child at her home, all the neighbours knew about it and some of the neighbouring women usually came to help her. If some strangers, like the Wise Men, came to see the baby, everybody around would know it. Would it attract attention to the mother and the child? Sure it would. To avoid this, the family had to leave the place where they lived before the baby was born.

If a woman gave birth to a child at some distant place with no other people but her husband around, though there was no problem with some strangers to come to see the baby, she run a risk to lose the baby or to die if anything went wrong.

Now, what would happen, if a woman gave birth to a child in an inn, where a lot of strangers were staying, and *then* there came some people to see the baby? Obviously, all the leaving the inn strangers would tell stories about the event they were witnesses to. Thus, the rumours would be spread rapidly all over the huge territory, which was exactly the most undesirable development of the situation.

What would be the way out? The answer is obvious: the family had to leave their home and the birth had to occur in some hidden place, which was close to people, but not among them. Thus, we get the answer: the birth had to take place in the stables!

The answer may seem weird, but it is the right answer. The procedure of birth would go without attracting any attention as animals gave birth too and screamed and shouted loudly as well. No strangers would know about the newly born baby. Still, the place was warm, clean and easy to reach to those who knew about it.

Then, what is most important for a newborn baby? – Cleanness, warmth and nutrition. Where could be all these things easily found and provided? – It may sound as a paradox, but all the things were really easy to establish in stables. There was a lot of hay and straw; thus there was no problem to keep the baby and the mother clean: the dirty staff could be removed at once being replaced by the clean one. There was a lot of fresh water as well. The place was dry and not cold as animals gave their warmth. The place was safe as there were no occasional people to come, and if they all of a sudden appeared nearby, the animals and the poultry would warn about them in good time.

Besides, the only milk healthy and suitable for a newborn baby but human's is that of a goat. There in old stables all the animals were kept together, and goats were very common domestic animals those days. So, you see, all the problems were solved: the baby would be safe and alive, and no one would pay any attention to it, even if the mother would die giving birth and there would be necessary to feed the baby with goat's milk.

Cases, when mother dies giving birth to her child, happen even now; obviously it happened more often those days. It was the first time for Mary to give birth, and nobody knew what to expect. Still, the baby had to be saved by all means. No matter if it would be a boy or a girl, the baby would be the descendant of the kings; and if the mother would die giving birth, it would be the last, the only representative of the royal family.

Luckily, everything went well. The baby was born normally, and the Wise Men came and gave the evidence of its birth, the birth of a new king of Jews, Jesus.

Gospel of Mathew (*2:11*) tells us,

> "When they had come into the house, they saw the young Child with Mary His mother, and fell down and worshiped Him."

Clear enough; they had to testify His birth, the birth of a new king though in exile, and behaved correspondingly. And then, after testifying that the newly born child was a genuine king, they had to swear their allegiance to Him; and we read,

> "And when they had opened their treasures, they presented unto Him gifts: gold and frankincense and myrrh." *(Ibid)*

Again everything was proper and right. The gifts were appropriate for a king as gold goes without saying, and so does frankincense and myrrh. The last two, apart from being really good to keep the skin clean, are typically used in the procedure of anointment of a king. Consequently, we conclude: there in the stables the newly born child Jesus was anointed as a king of Jews.

Scientists claim that in people's minds, the prosperity of a nation is directly connected with the prosperity of their kings [3]. In our case, it was not only a question of prosperity, but of the *survival* of the nation, which, in people's minds, was connected with the very existence of the king. That is why Jesus was anointed as a king immediately after His birth: the event was of an extreme importance to Jewish people.

Pay attention to the following: according to the gospels, there was *Mary* who showed the baby to the Wise Men, but not Joseph. The peculiarity of the situation, though, is that according to the tradition, which some places still exists, especially in Jewish and similar cultures, women having menstruation or after giving birth are considered to be "unclean" and must stay away from men. It was (and some places it still is) forbidden to men even to see women in such state. During this period, even husbands were not allowed to see their own wives, not mentioning strangers. Not allowed and forbidden?.. – Well... If we think of royal families... They were exceptions; for them there were other rules to follow; the rules for royals worked the opposite way. Too many things depended on genuineness of their children[5].

With the time being, the relation and the origin from King David was removed from Mary and attributed to Joseph. I consider it might be done following the general rules of inheritance: the hairs were determined exclusively among members of the family of male gender. In the meaning of a storyteller it should have been Joseph who was the most important member of the family – thus, it should have been him who was the hair of the kings; such situation looked right and was much easier to understand.

I can accept though, there could be other reasons for forging the story of the Mary's origin. For example, it might be done with the purpose to protect her, the real descendant of the royal family and bearer of the royal blood in case of an attack on the family. Joseph was replaceable, Mary wasn't.

As for the star of Bethlehem... Well, *that* was a coincidence.

Notes

1. In the Constitution Ineffabilis Deus of 8 December, 1854, Pius IX pronounced and defined, that the Blessed Virgin Mary "in the first instance of her conception, by a singular privilege and grace granted

by God, in view of the merits of Jesus Christ, the Saviour of the human race, was preserved exempt from all stain of original sin."

2. The holiday of Easter existed long time before Christ though known under other names. In many countries and cultures, it was celebrated as a beginning of a new year.

3. Mathew 1:18-24; Luke 1:26-55, 2:4-5

4. That is one of the versions. Later, we discuss another one.

5. That is one of the explanations of special attitude towards Mary, Jesus' mother, and the moment of His birth. Later, we discuss some other aspects of the problem.

5

Origin

Taking into consideration everything we discussed in the previous chapter, the conclusion, that neither Mary nor Joseph was of "common origin", seems to be obvious. In other words, the version with Joseph being a poor carpenter from Nazareth goes to pieces.

You see, if Mary really was a descendant of House of King David, she definitely could not be a common ill-bread girl. Even if she was an orphan and grew up in a foster-family[1], this family had to be appropriate for the descendant of the royal family to grow up in.

The members of the family had to be well-bred for to give the girl suitable upbringing and education. Under all circumstances, there was a hope that she would marry a proper man and bring her people to prosperity. The family had to be prosperous, but not too wealthy for the girl to grow up healthy, but not being envied or noticed by the unwanted people, whose attention could be a threat to her life. Apart from this, the family had to be worth the trust; otherwise the girl's life would be in danger. In other words, the girl should grow up healthy, safe and sound to guarantee survival of the royal family and continuation of the bloodline.

Why would that well-bred and good-educated girl from a well-being family have to marry a poor old man? Even if the man indeed was as righteous as described in gospels, I would never believe it. I would rather accept that Joseph was something quite different from being a poor old carpenter whom we used to see. I'm not sure if some love took place when this marriage was arranged, but I'm absolutely sure that Joseph was chosen to marry the girl because of the certain characteristics he possessed; i.e., *he was appropriate for her.*

It is possible that neither Joseph nor Mary had a great fortune. Maybe they had something, but taking into consideration that the family lived unnoticed by the society for a long time and did it, most surely, incognito, i.e., without declaring the real origin of the members of the family, we may conclude, that the money of the family was not significant, or that the family was limited with the access to their money.

Could it be that such mode of living of the family was caused by the political situation in the country? Definitely yes. The members of the royal family had to live "in exile" in their own country being unrecognized among other people. They had to do it to survive; the political situation in the country dictated it. If they wouldn't, Roman authorities would threaten their lives.

Some time ago, there were published documents claiming that Mary, Jesus' mother, was raped by a Roman legionary, and Jesus was born as a result of the act. The scripts even gave the name of the legionary: Panthera, which apparently was quite a common name for Roman soldiers. Is it possible? Absolutely. That time a Jewish uprising in Galilee took place; and as we know, raping was quite common among men participating in military actions.

Probably, it was then, during the uprising, Mary's family was killed. In this case, it is clear, why Mary was all alone, i.e., no father, mother, sisters, or brothers were mentioned. Still, if they were mentioned some place, who can say for sure, that they belonged to her genuine, but not to her foster-family? When we take into consideration the typical size of a family – usually numerous, which was traditional for the culture and the time – and the relations usually existed between members of the family – typically very close – we must admit, that existence of a girl without *any* family hardly can be considered as normal. The supposition, that Mary's family was killed during the uprising, sounds as a possible and logical explanation of her staying alone.

As a result, we once again return to the situation, when of the whole family there was only one girl left alive.

And then – and that is absolutely logical! – those who were responsible for the existence and wellbeing of the royal family arranged her marriage. They found a proper and reliable man who had to take care of her and her coming child, and Mary got married. In this way, she and her coming child became protected.

The man – Joseph – belonged to Zealots that was highly respected community in ancient Judea. Getting married to the girl he confirmed his social status, and their common children would be able to take a good place in the society. As for her first child – well, the boy had to stay a bit separately having another father. And that is the exact situation we meet in gospels: Joseph and his children stayed separately from Jesus, who was much closer to His mother than to any other member of the family.

If Mary was raped indeed, it could also be one of the reasons for the family to move from the original place of their living. Attitude towards children born as a result of raping is rare friendly, and the mother is usually blamed for the event. Moving of the family far from the place of their living would prevent the rumours and exclude the negative attitude of neighbours. People forget reasons very easily, but they remember the attitudes for a very long time.

By the way, here we find another reason for the history of Immaculate Conception to appear. The purpose is obvious: to clean the names of the mother and the child. The task would be of primary importance if the mother indeed belonged to the House of David, but if not... Just think, what was the necessity to invent an excuse for the birth of a child, if it was born in marriage, and especially, if his father was of such noble origin as it was claimed by the book of generation, i.e., if he was a descendant of House of King David? No, in this case inventing of the story of Immaculate Conception makes no sense at all.

In the long run, if Mary indeed was the only descendant of the royal family, it would makes no difference to the people if Mary got married at all, whom she got married, how she became pregnant, or who was the father of her coming child. The most important thing still remained the same: it was *her* who was the mother of the child. Her, Mary, the representative of the House of David, the only one bearer of the royal blood, the only hope of Jewish people to revive.

In this case, the wish to separate the child from the husband of his mother is natural and well-grounded: it only reflected the real situation. More than that, if later Mary and Joseph had common children, they should have been of no much interest for the contemporaries, I mean for those who obtained the information of the real state of the events. And this is the situation we meet in gospels: Jesus' brothers and sisters were of no interest at all to those who told the story. If we keep in mind the scene in stables with worshipping Jesus by the Wise Men and *"gold and frankincense and myrrh"* used for that, everything comes to the right places. It was *Jesus* who was their anointed sovereign, *His* children would be of interest, but all the others were of no importance.

And now, as you see, we have returned to the picture "Virgin Mary and the child", which about we already talked in the previous chapter and which seems to be of much more importance to the Catholic than to the Orthodox Church. Now, when we recollect, that the

Catholic Church was established by Peter (Simon) – Galilean and, like Jesus, Jew by origin –it becomes clear, that to him and to the other disciples, who were also Jews, the moment of Jesus' birth and His close connection to His mother meant much more than to Greeks, who probably knew nothing about the history and sufferings of Jewish people and, actually, were not really interested in it.

Of course, believers of the Orthodox Church celebrate Christmas and respect Virgin Mary, who according to the tradition bears the name "She-Who-Gave-Birth-to-a-God"[2]; but the attitude to the events differs much from that existing in the Catholic Church tradition.

There in traditions of the Catholic Church, we cannot find explanations, why the moment of Jesus' birth was of such great importance; why the same great importance had Jesus' connection to His mother, Mary, despite her being married to Joseph and despite the leading role of men in the family and the society of that time; and why it was so important to His mother to be *a virgin* giving birth to her son. Actually, it was thus important then, that even now, after 2000 years, the cult of Virgin Mary and the child still remains one of the most important and honourable cults in the traditions of Catholic Church.

Now, we know the answer: it was important to clean the name of Mary and genuine king Jesus, and so the tale of Immaculate Conception was invented. Besides, it would be too shameful to people to accept that the 50% of the blood in the veins of their genuine king belonged to someone, and not just to someone, but to an enemy; and even not to just an enemy, but to someone lowest in the rank of the importance of the enemies. As for the Greeks – for them it was insignificant whose blood flows in the Jesus's veins, thus the tale of Immaculate Conception became of not so much interest in the Orthodox Church traditions.

But let us return to Mary' and Joseph.

I have no intention to discuss now, what features the man had to possess to become a husband of a girl, who was the heir of the House of King David. There are just a couple of points, which I would like to mention in this connection.

First, this man had to be one of those who attract no attention to himself, i.e., he was a rather ordinary-looking man. Otherwise, people might pay too much attention to him and to his family, and lives of the mother and the child could be in danger. Second, he had to be a well-to-do person to provide the suitable living conditions for the family and to guaranty survival of its members. And the third and the most important thing: he had to be clever enough to cope with the task of guarding and protection of the woman and the child, whose survival were extremely important to the whole nation. As history shows us, he managed his task brilliantly.

Moreover – pay attention, it is important! – when the political situation in the country was changed and it became possible for the family to return to their native place, Joseph never did it. Gospels tell us: Joseph made a decision and, together with his family, moved to Nazareth (*Mathew 2:19-23*). That means, that Joseph preferred to settle down in a foreign place where there were neither relatives nor friends and nobody could possibly help the family. However we all know, that establishing of new contacts is always much more difficult than restoring those existed in advance. The only explanation of the strange decision is that Joseph, by all means, wanted to avoid any attention to his family and had enough resources to begin at a new place.

Gospel of Mathew (*2:19-20*) tells us, that Joseph *was told* to act this way. In the next chapter, we'll analyze it in details.

As a result of all the above mentioned, instead of the family of a poor carpenter from Nazareth, we see a family consisting of well-educated people, rather but not too wealthy, probably but not obligatory belonging to Jewish aristocracy. You see, Mary's husband anyway had to be worth her.

I admit as a possibility that Joseph indeed worked as a carpenter – well, he had to do something for living. At the same time, he obviously had to find the position allowing him (and the family) to be unseen among others in the society.

Who was Joseph indeed? I wish I knew it!.. Just imagine, he was the man bearing the task of an incredible importance, which was a top-secret mission at the same time, and still he managed to keep himself in the background. There were not many places in the scripts telling us about him, but even those pieces of information are enough to make us understand, that he devoted all his life to the task of serving the child and His mother. First – the mother, and then – the child. Yes, they led a family life with Mary and they had common children, and still…

Well, I think he was an outstanding person: well-educated, well-bred, and really clever; otherwise he definitely would not be able to perform the mission.

And now, I believe, you understand why I wrote, that there were obviously the parents, who taught little and later young Jesus to behave Himself in such a way that would make it possible for Him to function in the society without attracting any special attention. That was the mode of living of the whole family, you see.

History shows us that to a certain point Jesus really did it, but then…

Notes

1. As far as I know, nobody has ever proved or refuted the supposition.

2. Богородица (*Russian*)

6

Angels

If everything I wrote until now was irrelevant to any miracles, now, there comes the time to talk about them. Although – what can be more mysterious and enigmatic than inner world of a person and the real world we all live in?

Anyway, let us return to Jesus. As we agreed, He was born and grew up exactly as all the other children around Him; otherwise we would hear about it.

Nevertheless, I would never believe that the boy, who meant so much to His people, would be left to grow up "as it goes," and there would be no observers to check what was happening to Him. Being anointed as a king in His very cradle, this child was obviously much too important to be left and forgotten like that.

Now – pay attention! Reading gospels, we all the time run across some strange characters, who typically carried out the most important missions; I mean Angels. There are quite a lot of places in gospels mentioning them. The really interesting thing, though, is that their tasks were of most earthly origin and importance. They, for example, comforted pregnant Mary and arrange the marriage between her and Joseph – and Joseph obeyed them (*Luke 1:26-38; 2:5*). They informed Joseph about the necessity to leave the country and to move to Egypt – and did it in time. Talking to Joseph, they, at the same time, mentioned that when the dangerous time would pass and it would be safe to return back to the country, they would give him a message about it as well – and they really did it when King Herod died.

The next thing, I want you to pay attention to, is the strange history we have already mentioned, a strange tale about an overcrowded inn where there was no place for the family with a woman going to give birth to her child (*Luke 2:7*). Was the inn really overcrowded so badly that there was not possible to find a place – *any place* to the poor woman? Isn't it more likely that the family was placed in the stables *on purpose*? Was it done to prevent her and the coming baby from being noticed by extraneous spectators, which we talked about in the previous chapters? And the legend was invented later to explain the presence of the woman and her newly born child in such an inappropriate place, which contradicted all the norms and traditions. As for the owner of the inn – maybe, he was *paid* to do it? Or, maybe, he had *to obey the orders?*

When giving birth women used to get help – and in the most cases there are women to help each other; but there was not a single woman to help Mary when she was giving birth to her first child.

I consider as an impossible situation that there were no women in the inn, especially taking into consideration that, according to the gospels, the inn was overcrowded – and not only by men, I suppose. There *had* to be women among visitors, as well as among those working at the inn. Women should have been among the members of the family of the owner of the inn, at least one woman, his wife.

I have already mentioned that in Jewish culture and those similar to it, there was a tradition which still exists some places: women in certain state, i.e., after giving birth to a child, are considered to be "unclean" and no men were allowed to see them. Besides, in case of necessity – especially in connection with the "girls" problems – every woman searches help from *a woman*, not from a man, and every woman helps her sister.

Still, there in the gospels we read about the opposite situation: not a single woman existed in Mary's surrounding when she was giving birth to her first baby, just men. *Only* men. They were Joseph, the Wise Men, and later shepherds. That is something that would enormously contradict *all* the existing traditions.

Why it was like that? – The answer is obvious: to keep the secret – at least to the moment when everything important was over and *those-who-make-the-decisions* had made them.

Here again, Angels are mentioned. It was an Angel, who informed the shepherds about the newly born child and ordered them to come to see the baby (*Luke 2:9-20*). Now, there comes another question: why he, I mean, the Angel, did it? Wasn't it because there had to be some outside witnesses whose task was to spread the message and to inform Jewish people about the newly born King? Or was it done in order to prevent unwanted rumours as shepherds anyway would learn about the mother and the baby in the stables? It is well-known nowadays: if people are given explanations in advance, i.e., before questions arise in their minds, first, it is not sure the questions arise in general, and second, the explanations provoke much less discussions about the item than the perplexity resulting in questions and rumours.

Anyway, no matter which explanation we choose, all the activities of Angels look like deliberate actions of the people, who perfectly well understood both: the political situation in the country and psychology of people. This means, that we again came to the possibility of existence of an organization or a group of people, most likely, not numerous and kept under deep secret, which members could easily communicate all the strata of society from a palace of a king to the camp-fire of shepherds – actually, we read about it in gospels. We see the organisation that had possibility and resources to obtain the reliable information and to use it properly as, e.g., sending it to the place where it was needed – and did it fast! We see the organisation, members of which were able to make the decisions considering lives and activities of other people, *who obeyed them.*

The conclusion is astonishing and yet… Let us try to check it once again; but this time we'll go another way round.

When a person lives in exile or moves to live to a new place far from home, he typically needs much more money for survival, than when living at the native place - especially at the beginning. At home, the person has his place to live (possibly, his home), the place to work and the permanent occupation (apparently, his own business). Apart of that, people usually have a network of personal and professional contacts, which makes the life a lot easier. At a foreign place, on the contrary, there are much fewer possibilities to make money, especially at the very beginning, and the expenditures are usually more remarkable especially at the first time after arrival.

First of all, it is necessary to find a place to live, which is usually more expensive than when living at home. Second, living at the same place for a long time, people usually have all the necessary household utensils. Moving to another place, people have to begin from the very beginning, as it is simply impossible to take all the necessary for normal life household utensils with them. Besides, it is necessary to buy food and clothes. Living at the same place, especially, for a long time, people, as a rule, have some extra supplies and remnants that could be used in the case of necessity. All these things had to be bought again at the new place soon after arrival. That is why, generally speaking, it is much cheaper and much more convenient to stay home than to move and to settle down at a new place.

All the problems become even more serious, if it is not a single man, but a family to move; and especially the one with a baby, or a child, or children. Children, as you know, need special care and more or special food; besides, they grow up quickly and need more clothes than adults, even in warm climate.

Even if the person had speciality which was demanded everywhere the situation would be the same. Let us check what situation would look like if the person was a carpenter.

To work as a carpenter, the man needed instruments and materials. He had either to carry them with him, suppose, from his native place, or to buy them again at the place of the destination. Second, there might be other persons performing the same type of the job whatever it was. When there is a need there are people to make the work to satisfy it, which is obvious. Consequently, if the person succeeded being a carpenter at his native place, it did not obligatory mean that he would succeed in doing the same job some other place.

Yes, it is possible to work as a hired worker and sometimes it is the only way possible to provide the family with food and supplies; but who would say for sure that it is easier and better paid at a new place than when living at the native place?

Sure, there may be different reasons making people to move from one place to another; but if you ask any emigrant of our time, I am sure, 98% of them confirm my words.

As a consequence, there comes the question, *why* Mary and Joseph left their native place if there was *nothing special* about them? We may re-formulate the question: *why* were Mary and Joseph *warned* about the danger, if they were nothing else, but common people? Why, among all the people, there was *the only one* family to be warned?

You see, again, it does not work. There *had* to be a reason making this particularly family special, the reason, why they were warned to leave in time.

Next. Where did Mary and Joseph get their money from? We had agreed that they belonged at least to the middle class, i.e., they had possessions. How much money and what possessions did they take with them when escaping? I mean, did they take *all* their possessions with them? Well, I doubt it. Obviously, they had no much time to pack, and they run a risk to be robbed during the journey. Could it be that they got money from time to time from the same *Angels* who arranged the marriage, who warned them about the danger, and who continued to help Mary and Joseph further on with their family life? Might it be, that the Wise Men were not just occasional strangers but *some of the Angels as well*?

Taking into consideration all the details of the history, we have already discussed, I should say, I definitely think so.

Maybe it was like that: Joseph left most of their belongings and trusted the money to the Angels – let us use that name further on – taking only the absolutely necessary things and limited amount of money with him. Later, the Angels sold the house (and I do believe they had a good one) and delivered the money to Joseph when meeting the family at the place of birth of Jesus and / or at the final point of destination.

You see, it is much less dangerous to travel, when the travelling person is a priest. Nobody pays any special attention to him; even robbers do not do it, as it is common knowledge: such people never have any decent possessions with them. Well, of course, there may be some exceptions, but usually the attitude and the situation is as described above. If it works like this nowadays, we can be absolutely sure, it worked even better those old days – and many examples presented in literature confirm it.

Actually, there was one possibility more. Angels could provide Joseph and Mary with the money taken from the treasures of the legendary kings, King David and King Solomon. The legend of their enormous treasures survived throughout the centuries and exists even nowadays; as for the treasures, they have never been found yet. Is it possible that the knowledge of the treasures was kept in secret by the same organization of Angels, members of which came to the Jesus' cradle to testify His birth? If so, it becomes clear: these treasures could and had to be used to support the family during the journey and later on. The treasures were needed to protect the king and to guarantee His survival.

What kind of people would form the organization guarding the treasures and the secrets of the royal family? It seems to be obvious: the organisation had to be formed of people, who, first, were used to be well organised, and second, who had access to the treasures. Hence either these people belonged to the army and were direct guardians of the treasures, or they were priests. As for the army, these people, as a rule, were much more interested in *using* the treasures they could reach, than in hiding, guarding, and saving them for somebody in the future – especially when there was no one to pay them for that. But if we think about representatives of a church – well, that type of behaviour seems most likely to be suitable for them.

By the way, the name "Angels" sounds quite appropriate for an organisation attributed to a church. The full name of it could possibly sound like, e.g., "Angels of Rescue and Protection", "Guarding Angels", "Angels of God", or "Angels of Yahweh".

The organization was not numerous; otherwise, it would be impossible to keep the secret. And finally, the organization had to be formed and kept in deep secret; it had to be a top clandestine organization. If not, its members were running a risk to be caught one by one by those willing to find and to use the legendary treasures, by treasure hunters.

There are no scripts confirming this supposition of mine. If one day, such scripts will be found, I am sure, they will be found at the same place where the treasures were hidden. The scripts describing the last days of the dynasty definitely lie together with the treasures of the dynasty.

7

Knowledge

The time passed, Jesus grew up, and everything seemed to be normal. Then, all of a sudden, problems began to appear. The outrages abilities of Jesus began to show themselves.

I believe it all began with His night dreams. We all dream when sleeping. Sometimes, we can remember our dreams and share our visions with those close to us: our friends and members of our families. Occasionally, we admit our dreams to be prophetic, especially when looking backward.

It is obvious, that at the ancient times, dreams meant much more to people than they do now. The life was simpler, and the pace of it was much slower comparing to that of contemporary society.

What was even more important, there were fewer sources of information comparing to those we have nowadays, and the pressure of information was significantly less. Correspondingly, the people were much more concentrated on their feelings, impressions, and inner lives. Hence we may undoubtedly assume that at the ancient times people paid much more attention to their dreams and feelings than we do it now. And the dreams of *this* boy were really *special*.

These dreams began to appear approximately at the same time when the *special* abilities of Jesus, i.e., ability to heal, His clairvoyant talent, His ability to mind-reading and His ability to hypnotic suggestion, began to show themselves.

There is an apocryphal script named "The Infancy Gospel of Thomas". Researches claim this particular script of no historical value, but apart from the script there are no other descriptions of early days of Jesus and His actions as a child. There in the script, we can read of miracles performed by Jesus when being a child. The miracles were astonishing, frightening, and weird.

I myself would definitely not believe the stories described in "The Infancy Gospel of Thomas". You see, if Jesus indeed acted just a bit like described there, i.e., performing wicked miracles; first, we would not have had the date of the beginning of His *special activity*, i.e., when He began preaching; and second, if Jesus being a child performed at least some of the things described there in the script, He would be punished by authorities long time before He became an adult. People would never accept such a neighbour.

Most likely, these stories appeared much later, when people wanted to reconstruct the story of Jesus' life. The time had passed; rumours, describing His life, His death, and His resurrection, circulated among people already for a long time. Long time passed since the days of His childhood, and people who could remember His life and especially His childhood were gone long time ago. Those who were interested in Jesus and His life tried to imagine, what could possibly happen in His childhood? Knowing the tales of the last actions of Jesus, they tried to imagine, what could it be in the beginning of His life for to end it like this? That was the source of the incredible histories written in "The Infancy Gospel of Thomas". You remember, we all like good stories no matter what century we live in.

Anyway, some strange things definitely began to happen in early years of Jesus, which we already mentioned in the previous chapters. Still, I am sure, no matter what abilities showed Jesus in His childhood, for Mary and Joseph they were of no surprise at all. They knew Jesus was through His mother a descendent of the kings who were unspeakably wise and had abilities beyond all imagination; that claimed legends they believed. The only task for Mary and Joseph, as they understood it, was to provide Jesus with the possibility to grow up safely and to protect Him from the danger; first of all, from being *noticed and seen*. To achieve the goal, they had to teach young Jesus to behave Himself exactly the same way as all the other children of His age. Let us not forget, the Massacre of Innocent was arranged especially to eliminate Him, Jesus.

That is another reason why I do not believe the stories of the miracles performed by Jesus in His early years. Of course, there could be some strange events, but if they really took place as described, the rumours would soon come to the authorities and provoke the interested in the child, which had to be fatal for Him. Happily enough, the things were different; and Jesus grew up without major problems.

While Jesus was still a baby, Mary and Joseph's task of primary importance was to protect Jesus against the authorities. With the time being, when Jesus grew op and especially when He became a teenager, their major task became to protect Jesus first of all from Himself. The task was really difficult, because once appeared, paranormal abilities usually continue to increase and become stronger with the time being; plus teenagers have their own behavioural problems, which we all know about. That is why Mary and Joseph had to teach Jesus to behave Himself properly for not to be sized from the society and *do not attract attention*. How? – First of all, by not telling His playmates and people around about the things He knew or saw including those of His dreams and visions.

And Jesus really had them: dreams and visions telling about the things, people usually never think about; I am more than sure of it.

It is there from much later He got His ideas about the structure of the world, about what a church should and should not do and be like, about the future that was inevitable for Him… as long as He believed His visions. Now again, we broach the item we are to discuss later. Let's take one step at a time.

Well, both Mary and Joseph accepted all the *special things* about Jesus as normal and taken for granted. Besides, as I have already mentioned, when something happens every now and then, people get used to it very soon and pay no attention when it happens again.

But what about the Angels, i.e., priests responsible for the life and wellbeing of young Jesus? For them, I can imagine, after some quiet period, the problems appeared as a bolt from the blue.

You see, one thing is *to tell* the stories about miracles, which took place somewhere else long time ago being performed by a legendary person. The other thing is to *believe* these stories. And quite another pair of shoes is to listen and to believe stories of miracles performed by a child, whom you know from the very moment of his birth.

What priest is brave enough to confirm that the power demonstrated by a child goes from the God but not form the Devil? Even nowadays? Who, among priests, has enough power and courage to declare it? Especially if there were some vague moments as for the origin of the child?

These sad words were said not by me and not now, but I completely agree with them,

> "A prophet is not without honor, save in his own country
> and in his own house…" *(Mathew 13:57).*

Pay attention to the following: not a single supporting Jesus priest was mentioned in gospels. Several times Jesus went to synagogue to talk to people, but the result was negative each time.

Actually, there was only one moment "joining" Jesus to a church (but not to the ruling one!), namely, it was the ceremony of baptism performed by John the Baptist; the ceremony which had never existed before and which, I definitely mean it, was established by one person for this purpose only.

Why did Jesus come to perform the ceremony to the man, who was well-known because of his weird behaviour? If you choose to ask me about it, I answer, "It happened because Jesus was pressed by something freighting, something awful, and got the idea how to get rid of it. The idea seemed to be weird, but as it came exactly the same way, as usual, i.e., in His dream, He followed it. Or, maybe, He did it just because He was desperate and couldn't see any other way out. But all that would happen much later and we talk about it in details. Now, we'd better return to Jesus' childhood and to priests responsible for His wellbeing.

I do not think the Angels kept an eye on Jesus permanently. More likely, they came from time to time to visit the family. During these visits, they checked if the boy was healthy, perhaps, supplied the family with some money if necessary, and left again. As Mary and Joseph believed that all the *strange* things happening to Jesus were normal to Him, they obviously didn't feel it necessary to tell the Angels about the trivia. Most likely, it was just a coincidence that they mentioned it, or it was something happened during a visit of one of the Angels. But when they, I mean Angels, learned about these "trivia"...

You see, there is one more nuance of the situation. It is allowed to be a wise man and a healer to *a king*, but not to *a boy*, who was born nobody knows whom from, meaning His father, and grows up just in front of your eyes. *A king* may be a worrier. But *a king must not* be a conjurer or a fortune-teller. These functions are normally performed by his advisers: priests, wise men, or some *strange people* who might come to the king and give him a word of advice if asked. It is *up to the king* to decide whether to listen to them or not. That is *in his* power to make the decisions; but *to know and to understand* things, especially those of divine origin, is in the authority of priests and wise men. Very long time ago, as legends tell us, there lived kings that could perform all that, but they do not live now, not here, and by all means it is not this particular boy, who has only one merit, namely, the pure blood of His mother running into His veins. As for His behaviour...

It is only in legends kings healed people by laying their hands upon their heads. In reality, healers, usually, do not make fortune and glory by helping people.

I have no doubts that Jesus seriously discredited Himself in the eyes of Angels by choosing the way of life of a healer. He should become a warrior and help His people against power of Rome, but instead, He began to perform something, which was absolutely inappropriate for a king and the future ruler of the nation.

Well, of course He *is* of royal blood, no doubt about it: He is a son of His mother, and He is the anointed king. Consequently, it is necessary to wait, maybe His son will be better to fulfil the obligations and comes up to the expectations of the people. People of Israel are used to wait long...

8

Baptism

Then, there came a moment that drastically changed Jesus' life. He left everything He did before and began to preach the new belief. He did it in spite of His deep understanding of the consequences of His actions.

Why did He do it? What was the cause of His actions? Historians claim, that time there was a lot of people, profits, preaching new beliefs; so, maybe Jesus came under the influence of one of them? – No, the gospels give us quite an opposite picture: Jesus began His activity as a preacher all of a sudden by coming to John the Baptist demanding to baptize Him.

Actually, when thinking of Jesus' baptism a lot of questions appear.

1. John the Baptist was not a priest, which means that, strictly speaking, he was not authorised to talk on behalf of God and to administer the sacrament. *He himself was not baptized (Mark 11:27-33).*

2. John the Baptist preached "in wilderness" telling things, which would be considered *weird* even if heard nowadays. Nowadays, when we hear similar things proclaimed by people in the streets or some other public places, we usually shrug our shoulders thinking that these people are not quite adequate, meaning they, probably, have mental disorders.

3. Gospel of Mathews tells us about John the Baptist,

    "… there went out to him Jerusalem and all Judea and all the region round about the Jordan. And they were baptized by him in the Jordan…" *(3:5-6).*

    If it really was like that, why there was such a fuss made about Jesus being baptized by him? Apart from this, as we know, soon after the event, John the Baptist was brought to jail and put to death; and Jesus had to leave the town. That means that this event, I mean baptizing of Jesus, changed something in the whole situation around John the Baptist, which caused such reaction of the authorities.

4. And the last question here is: why do we know almost nothing about the people being baptized by John the Baptist? Yes, the gospels tell us there were lots of people coming to him searching for the procedure, but actually we have *no other names* but Jesus. *Why?*

I consider the situation to be like this: John *was* a weird man. Sure, he was one of those, who pays too high price for the paranormal abilities they possess. John the Baptist lived in a world of his own, or, as we say now, he was *not quite adequate*, meaning he was mentally disordered. We can see similar cases now, thus being mentally disordered John the Baptist was not an exception.

He lived "in wilderness", i.e., some distant place far from other people. Maybe the people did not want him to live in the neighbourhood; or, maybe, it was vice versa, John the Baptist was not able to live surrounded by people, who knows.

But you see, when people having paranormal abilities meet each other, they immediately recognize the abilities in one another. It is not obligatory if they choose to communicate, but they can't help *recognizing* another person having paranormal abilities. That exactly what happened when Jesus and John the Baptist first met: they immediately *understood* that either of them possessed the abilities. It was obvious though, the abilities of Jesus greatly exceeded those of John the Baptist. That was the reason for John to say,

> "I have need to be baptized by Thee, and comest Thou to me?" *(Mathew 3:14).*

Most likely, it was *Jesus* who let John the Baptist into the secrecy of baptism and told him what to do and how to behave when performing the rite. And it was definitely *Jesus* who put the deep meaning into the ceremony.

Could it be that Jesus saw the rite in one of His dreams? Maybe, we discuss it a bit later. As for John the Baptist, it seems as later, he continued to *repeat* the ceremony performed by him to Jesus, and that became a cause of the extra attraction for the people – especially if we take into consideration, that John the Baptist had already been known because of his weird behaviour and his homilies, which then became followed by the tales of the miracle that happened to Jesus after the ceremony of baptism. And rumours, as we know, used to spread rapidly; that is why *"Jerusalem and all Judea and all the region round about the Jordan"* were mentioned in the tale of John the Baptist.

After that, the number of people, coming to John the Baptist willing to be baptised and listening to his homilies, increased noticeably.

That was that, which changed the situation about John the Baptist and attracted attention of the authorities to him.

Actually, John the Baptist, made nothing *good* or *sweet*. Listen attentively to the words of his homily; it was not just a call to confess the sins. His homily was *aggressive* both in its style and in its meaning. Only once, there were soft tunes coming into it, it was when he talked to Jesus and about Him. That, I am sure, happened under the great influence of the personality of Jesus. That moment, the exceptional tolerance of inner philosophy of Jesus dominated the wildness of fantasies of John the Baptist.

After Jesus left, John the Baptist returned to his normal aggressive-denouncing state. He continued to "denounce" everybody and everyone and made it in such way that brought him to jail. Most probably, the people, attracted to him by the rumours of the miracle happened to Jesus after the ceremony, after listening to homilies of John the Baptist, began to act accordingly to them, i.e., became aggressive too; and that obviously made troubles in the nearby towns. As a result, the authorities became interested in that happening on the banks of the Jordan River. Their reaction was easy to predict: they arrested the initiator of the troubles, John the Baptist. As we may say now, the authorities act exactly the same way in the similar situations regardless of the century, of the country, and of the culture.

But then, there were no crowds of thankful people, that he baptized, who should expectedly come to demand his freedom. Vice versa, there were people wanting John the Baptist to be beheaded; and because of his arrest, Jesus had to leave the town.

Actually, it makes no wonder. If a person nowadays, standing in a street or some public area, begins to declare things similar to those declared by John the Baptist, even if *not* doing it the same aggressive manner, people very soon call either police or ambulance. The similar attitude and the same actions cause the same reaction.

As for the quoted part about people coming to John to be baptized, it was obviously written much later to explain why Jesus came to John the Baptist in the first place, and why the ceremony was performed. Here we meet the situation when the cause and the effect changed their places due to the storytellers – and we meet the situation not only once.

Baptism itself appeared as a modified ceremony of ablution existed in Roman and Jewish[1] cultures, which came from ancient ceremony of initiation, existed in most cultures. Jesus only changed it a bit and filled it with the new meaning.

Judge for yourself: in general, initiation is a rite of passage ceremony marking change in a person's status, i.e., changing the person's belonging to a certain social, sexual, coming-of-age or any other group and joining to another group of people. Many times, as a result of the procedure of initiation, the person joins the group obtaining certain esoteric knowledge, i.e., the sacral information not available to uninitiated people. Correspondingly, the members of the initiated group get due to that higher social status than "not enlightened" people.

The main stages of initiation typically are:

1. refusal of a neophyte of his previous life;
2. intermediate state of the person being initiated, i.e., the state "without status";
3. return to the social life of the person in a new status, often under a new name that symbolize his new life acquired as a result of the initiation, i.e., a new essence of the character of the person.

The most common scenario of initiation is the symbolic death of the person being initiated followed by his "rebirth" possessing new quality (status).

Now, let us examine the ceremony of baptism.

1. According to the teachings of the Church, baptism ceremony means that the person "dies for the sensual, sinful life, and is reborn from the Holy Spirit in the lives of spiritual, holy". Gospel of John tells us,

    "Unless a man be born of water and of the Spirit, he cannot enter into the Kingdom of God," *(3:5).*

2. Immersion in water or purification by pouring water over a person or his hands existed in cultural traditions of many peoples of antiquity: Chaldeans, Phoenician, Egyptians, Persians, partly among Greeks and Romans. The procedure had special importance in the sense of not only physical, but also moral purification; i.e., the personality was being "washed up". Moreover, according to the traditions of most of the cultures, the world of dead is separated from the world of living by *a river.* Correspondingly, dipping into the water, which later was modified into its pouring or sprinkling, symbolises death of the person and his moving into another world, the world of spirits. The very first ceremony of baptism, i.e., baptism of Jesus, occurred *in the river* Jordan. To this day, the Christian ceremony of baptism occurs with the use of water: threefold immersion in water occurs in the Orthodox Church in rite of baptism, sprinkling and pouring of water are used in the Catholic and other Christian Churches.

3. After being baptized, a person received a new name[2] and a special cross for permanent wearing as a symbol of the sacrament ceremony performed. The new name could be the same as the old one or not coincide with it; it could be even used together with the old name, which actually is of no importance for us now. The important thing

though is, that it is believed, that after being baptized by the God's grace, the person is cleaned from all his sins; he becomes justified and sanctified and enters the church, as in some new "promised land, boiling honey and mammals." In other words, he returns to public life in a new status, which is rather higher and unreachable for uninitiated.

There is one considerable thing that differs baptism from all the other rites of initiation: after being baptized, neophyte did not receive any appreciable material benefits. Instead, after being baptized, people began to run a risk of massacres and persecutions. Isn't it the reason why it took so long time to Christianity to spread? The only privilege got by people when joining the teaching of Christianity was consolation, promise of support from heavens, new moral rules, which I consider to be of great importance, and the hope for the future prosperity in Kingdom of God.

Was this acquisition worth all the persecutions suffered by Christians and all the blood spilled in the name of Christianity? Honestly, if there was not for the new morality, which little by little changed our world into the one we know now, I would doubt to say "yes". And even taking into consideration that the new rules of morality were received, I would say that the price paid for that by humanity was too high.

Notes

1. Mikvah.

2. It is interesting, though, if Jesus had another name before He was baptized. Could it be that He had quite a different name, and that is the reason why we can't find any reliable information about His early years? Maybe it is not a coincidence that in the Orthodox Church, *a secular name* still exists. The name is used *in a world*, as well as the name under which the person was baptized. In the Catholic and other Christian traditions, though, a person gets his name *only* in the rite of baptism.

9

Visions

Would you like to know, where from Jesus took His ideas? Why did all that begin so suddenly? I do not mean historical standards, but for Jesus Himself. Shall I tell you?

The matter is following: the world, we all live in, is a closed unitary system. We may call the unity geo-, bio-, and noosphere[1], or energy-information field; particularly I prefer to call it simply "the System" [1]. All the words mean exactly the same: we live in a world where all the living creatures and events are connected to each other[2]. The important thing is that the whole our System exists in the state of comparative stability. When functioning, there appear different kinds of deviation in the System, but the general balance remains permanent – at least to the certain degree. Any significant violation of the balance inevitably leads to a backlash of the System. Its action would be aimed to restore the balance and would have the opposite polarity to the disturbing event. That is how the development, which we call a history of humankind, occurs. Here, I refer to humanity as a whole, without dividing it into countries, cultures, peoples, and civilizations [5].

When the total level of pain, suffering, violence, and other negative items of people's life significantly exceed average level acceptable for the System and causes the drastic disturbance of the balance, there appears the necessity to make adjustments aimed to remove the disturbance. These are the situations we usually call critical moments or turning points of the history of humankind. It is the time for new ideas to arise.

The information about the necessary changes "leaks" into the minds of people who have the ability to receive the information generated by the System, like those we mentioned in previous chapters. Later these "leaks" – or ideas – result in great migrations, rising of new kingdoms and religions, destroying of civilisations, etc. The process reminds the situation of water destroying a dam: at first slowly, in some places there appear small streams; then the streams become strong and numerous. Finally, the water washes away a large part of the dam; all the streams merge into one powerful track, which washes the dam away.

That's it! The leap forward is made; the quantity is changed into the quality and humanity has reached a new stage of its development. We need to notice here, that the water does not always flow into the desirable direction; the same may be said about the path of history.

Jesus was a huge "leak" in the dam. The informational flow of changes necessary for the subsequent development of humanity poured through the "leak" called Jesus with the enormous pressure; that was caused by His outrageous abilities to accept nonverbal information – also from the System[3].

Basing on the knowledge "sucked out" of the System, Jesus worked out His doctrine about what our world was and how it was functioning – we read about it in the ancient scripts. By His doctrine, Jesus united countless people: preachers that had ideas of their own – other "leaks of the dam", people that were not satisfied with the society and their place in it, and people just following "the main stream" of the powerful flow. He established the doctrine, later called Christianity, which destroyed many things and standards existed in the society before, and changed the world greatly transforming it into the one we live in now. Alas, the stream of history came not the exact way. It could be much better, if... Well, we'll talk about it later.

Actually, there were several turning points in the history of humanity. If we carefully study the time and the circumstances surrounding them, we'll notice:

1. Meaning historical standards, we have to admit that all the events were preceded by situations, where huge number of people was exposed to suffering. The level of prevailing cruelty surpassed all limits.
2. There appeared many leaders with more or less new ideas, and these leaders gained active followers.
3. There appeared *one* person, who became followed by huge mass of people, and that changed the course of history or the culture.
4. If such leader did not appear, there came natural calamities, like epidemics of plague, smallpox or cholera, and maybe natural disasters, taking lives of enormous amount of people. Still, as a result of the events, the course of history evolved; and the same may be said about the development of the culture.
5. All these events occur during periods of high solar activity, as it was proved by Professor A.L.Chizhevsky almost 100 years ago. The higher level of activity of the Sun is – the more victims occur and the more terrible circumstances accompany their deaths. Researches carried nowadays repeatedly confirmed the truthfulness of the theories, observations, and conclusions made by Professor A. L. Chizhevsky.

I need to add one more thing in this connection. Now, we live during a very difficult period. The activity of the Sun is high and still increasing. Scientists claim that during all the time of observations of the Sun, its activity has not yet been anything like it is now. They even do not dare to predict the level of its activity for the coming year. The situation in our world and society is corresponding: natural disasters, wars, rising of terrorism, the outbreak of epidemics; masses of people claiming themselves to be healers, clairvoyants, magicians, witches and sorcerers; an explosion of activity of different religions and sects and sudden rise of interest to them; people thirsting for healing, people seeking God… The dam, which I talked above, has definitely begun to leak; it seems to be on the edge of its collapse.

Scientists have proved that every living organism is a highly sensitive receiver reacting to changes in physical and chemical characteristics of the environment. The functioning of a living organism reacts to the fluctuations of its surrounding. As a result of these fluctuations, there occur changes in physical, mental, and emotional state, followed by diseases, and occasionally causing the death of the person. It is clear though, how else would the System influence us if not through our senses? We *are* a part of the System, you know.

There are some unique people, like those we talked about in chapters 2 and 3, who are able to perceive the direct "pushes" of the System. These people absorb the information like a sponge put in the water. They are never numerous, and levels of their perception differ much. Needless to say, that the quantity of the information and its quality greatly depends on the intellectual and educational level of the person receiving it.

Unfortunately, many people having mental disorders claim themselves to be like those above mentioned. Which is even sadder, many of those who indeed are capable to perceive the "hints" of the System suffer from various types of mental disorders. If only scientists could develop parameters, making it possible to determine what is caused by a disease and what is the pure information received from the System!..

In the whole history of humankind there were but a few people, who were able to accept the "tasks" given by the System without being least affected by mental disorder. One of those unique people was Jesus Christ.

I am absolutely sure: it all began not from the moment of baptism of Jesus and even not from His first meeting with John the Baptist. It all started with His dreams that were strikingly different from everything He had ever experienced before. These dreams returned again and again, and so did His visions. There were dreams denouncing the imperfection of the morality of the society and the wrong actions of the church; there were dreams showing the horrible future of people; dreams haunting Him and demanding *actions*... They were dreams caused by the increasing imbalance of the System.

There is one more thing worth mentioning here. When a person gets used to have prophetic dreams, at the same time, he or she gets used to take them into consideration in the everyday's life. It is true even now. I think you yourself might have had a prophetic dream at least once, or maybe you are used to get it regularly; thus you understand what I mean. As it is true now, we can be more than sure, it was exactly the same at the ancient times; and especially it was right considering the person having such exclusive abilities to absorb the information as Jesus.

Gospels claim that Jesus went to John the Baptist, who recognized Jesus and baptized Him in the waters of the Jordan River. After Jesus was baptized, the Holy Spirit descended upon Him, and then Jesus was tempted by devil.

Well, it sounds great and even seems to be logical – to the certain extent. But *only* to the certain extent. Let us regard the situation. The first question is, *why* or *what for* Jesus came to John the Baptist *in general*? Was it because Jesus wanted to listen to John's homily? Or maybe He did it because of curiosity, just for fun, or to spend some spare time of His? –I definitely do not think so.

Proceeding from the fact, that all the acting characters lived at the same place not far from each other, we may conclude that they knew each other, or at least *heard* about one another; particularly if we think about a person behaving himself as *weird* as John the Baptist. Being a person like he was described in gospels, it is clear, that John the Baptist and his actions, including his homilies, were well-known in the environs. Therefore it was well-known too, that in his homilies John the Baptist demanded from everyone to repent of their sins to be rescued "for the Kingdom of Heaven is at hand," *(Mathew 3:2)*. And *that* is the reason why Jesus came to him: He needed to be rescued.

What was that Jesus was searched to be rescued from? According to the gospels, nothing special happened that time in His life. The only horrible thing happened to Him close to the time of His baptism was His temptation performed by devil[4].

I have already mentioned, what an awful influence visions can make on the person; and if these visions come permanently and repeatedly, the pressure becomes unbearable. Therefore, when the System gives a "hint" in a dream or by an accidental phrase what to do to be rescued, you follow it immediately no matter how weird this way might seem.

Still, Jesus' personality is the cornerstone of understanding of the whole situation about Him. He *really* was an incredibly tolerant and positive-minded person, and he had a very strong feeling of responsibility. He was brought up to be a King, and His morality and the level of His responsibility were corresponding. There in the gospels, we find confirmation of the supposition. Even when Jesus literally fell down of exhaustion, He never refused people begging Him for help.

One awful night the tempter came to Him. Then, he came again… Jesus could never agree to his proposals; neither could He yield to temptation. Jesus *had already been used* to have His *special dreams* and visions; He already knew how much true these visions were; too well could He understand their meaning, and too seriously He took the spiritual world He saw in His dreams and visions. Jesus was exhausted by the torture. He suffered and searched for help. How? Perhaps, praying to God begging him for help, forgiveness, and support, as we all, probably, do when the time is hard and there is no other place for us to get help and support from. And the help came to Jesus. Once He had a vision in which He went to the river and... and then there was a rite of baptism later performed on Him by John the Baptist.

And it helped! After being baptized, Jesus felt relief; the devil left Him and never came again. The desirable result was achieved, because baptism, when eagerly wanted and taken seriously and sincerely, is a powerful source of defence of the inner world of a person.

Professor of Theology Per Bilde of Aarhus University, Denmark, means that Jesus was a Gnostic[5]; i.e., Jesus accepted the knowledge without further asking why and where from this knowledge came to Him. It is more than possible: when a person gets used to the truthfulness of his /her dreams and visions, especially believing in their divine origin, he accepts the knowledge without further questioning and hesitations.

The feeling of *knowing* is amazing. It is this feeling that makes a person to follow the dreams and inner impulses without extra thinking – especially if the person is used to it. This was the way Jesus regarded His world: reality, which was predicted and explained by His dreams, visions, and inner feelings; reality that He could and had to change.

All the actions of Jesus during the second half of His life were dictated by such understanding of the world, and this is the part of His life we know about.

The visit to John the Baptist followed by the ceremony of baptism was the first and the most visible action of Jesus. He came there in desperate attempt to escape the horror of His nightmares, searching for help, relief, and protection. The drastic measure worked; more than that, it was followed by the vision:

> "…And while He prayed the heaven was opened, and the Holy Ghost descended in a bodily shape like a dove upon Him, and a voice came from Heaven, which said, "THOU ART MY BELOVED SON; IN THEE I AM WELL PLEASED," *(Luke, 3:21-22).*

It was the beginning of real trust. After that, all the doubts, even if Jesus still had some, disappeared without a trace. Following His dreams, Jesus moved from one place to another, talked to people, healed them, *and taught* them. That was the time for Him to become visible.

I am sure, the pictures described in the gospels about the Holy Spirit Descent and temptations of Jesus are true storeys told by Jesus about what He saw and experienced – though in His vision, which could be of such clearness and strength, that people sometimes mix them with the reality even nowadays. The feelings, experienced during such visions, are extremely strong. Believe me, I have experienced it myself.

Obviously, the baptism and the following activity of Jesus were caused by His dreams or, as we may say, by the leaking dam of the System.

By the way, I can prove that the voice from heaven announcing *"THOU ART MY BELOVED SON; IN THEE I AM WELL PLEASED,"* was heard by only one person. It was just one peculiarity about it, which allows us to affirm that the voice was heard in a vision, therefore – by only one person.

You see, people living in different places have different accents. Even without thinking, we pay attention to the accent of the person when listening to the speech or talking to one. If we have heard the accent before, we can recognize it and guess where the person came from. It is really amazing to be able to guess the place of origin of the person. Even in the gospels, the first thing we learn about the people mentioned there is where they came from.

Because of the accent we recognise Russians, Poles, Danes, Frenchmen, Englishmen, Americans and others. Knowing the language better, we are able to locate the place of the origin more exact. Knowing English, we never mix an American with an Englishman or an Australian; knowing Russian, we never mix a Muscovite with a person from St.-Petersburg; Danes would have no doubt whether they talk to a Copenhagener or to someone from Fyn or Jutland.

Generally speaking, we may say that we distinguish people by their accents. However, the lack of the accent also attracts attention.

Now, here is the key question, *what accent* had the voice speaking from heaven?

Would you like to know what is wrong in the story? I can tell you that: *the only cases* when people cannot hear *any* accent and pay *no attention* to the pronunciation are when the person talks him-/herself or when the voice is heard in a dream. Consequently, the voice from Heaven was heard in a vision by only one person.

It's hard to say, who had the vision: was that John the Baptist, as gospels claim, or Jesus Christ, which I mean. It is possible, that after performing the rite of baptism, John the Baptist had the vision being deeply impressed by Jesus and the things He told him about. It is as well possible though, that it was *Jesus* who had the vision. Amazed, He told about it John the Baptist, who shared the impression and later might believe that it was *him*, who had the vision as well. You see, comparing to the other things John the Baptist used to talk about, this vision differed too much from all of them; but at the same time it was very much similar to those seen and described by Jesus.

It was the very first vision showing Jesus His special attitude to God. It was a shock, and that is why so much attention was paid to the event. Seeing it Himself, Jesus couldn't help believe the vision, and that was the reason why He told John the Baptist about it; and that is why He considered Himself to be the son of God. It was after this vision Jesus began to appeal to God, *"My Father"*. It was also accepted as a fact by John the Baptist, and later by the disciples, who definitely believed the words of Jesus and brought them to others, us including.

With the time passing, the story was changed a bit: the cause and the effect changed their places – we have already met the similar situation. But think, it is mere natural: from the point of view of the people living that time, a person *first* should become a Christian, and *only then* the one would be persuaded to renounce the belief.

Notes

1. The idea of noosphere belongs to Academician Vladimir Vernadsky (1863-1945). The noosphere is the third in a succession of phases of development of the Earth, after the geosphere (inanimate matter) and the biosphere (biological life), [4]. Interested in learning the theory are welcome to contact the author, the lectures can be provided

2. The concept is worked out by the author and presented under the name of the Theory of Alternative Understanding of the World. Interested in learning the theory are welcome to contact the author, the lectures can be provided.

3. Here, I need to add, that not every one of those receiving "the hints" of the System are lucky enough to succeed in bringing the message to public. Jesus was the lucky one – if we may say so taking into consideration the price He paid for that.

4. Mathew 4:3-10; Luke 4:2-11

5. From Greek: *gnōsis*, knowledge

10

Judas

Not so long time ago, there was found one more gospel. It was "The Gospel of Judas". But before sharing with you my thoughts caused by the text, I would like to attract your attention to the styles of gospels and to the language used in them.

When reading gospels, you can't help noticing how much their texts differ from each other by the language and by the style of presentation. On the one hand the cause of the differences is clear: there were several people involved into composing of the texts we read nowadays, specialists claim it doubtless. The original texts were influenced by time, interpreters, re-writers, and translators. And yet... And yet you would not mix an extract from Gospel of Luke with the one from Gospel of Matthew, Mark, James or any other gospel. The individual features of the person, who told the story originally maybe giving his name to the gospel, are partly reflected in the texts. Thus, comparing the text of The Gospel of Judas to canonical gospels, two things become obvious.

First, here in this particular gospel Jesus Christ talks differently. The specialists who analyzed and translated the original text claim His language to be rather sophisticated. Besides, Jesus talks about some things that had never been mentioned in any other gospel. He creates complicated philosophical constructions and images and explains them. In addition, He presents His thoughts in a different, much more sophisticated way.

In this aspect "The Gospel of Judas" resembles another apocryphal text: "The Gospel According to Mary Magdalene". In "The Gospel According to Mary Magdalene" the language is more sophisticated than in canonical gospels too, and here we meet the complicated philosophic constructions as well, although in "The Gospel of Judas" they are still more abstract. Images used in "The Gospel According to Mary Magdalene" are more "real" and easier to imagine comparing to those presented in "The Gospel of Judas."

There is one more thing that differs "The Gospel of Judas" from the other gospels. Here, we meet Jesus acting not *as an icon* but *as a living person*. We never saw anything like that in any other gospel yet. Jesus makes jokes, He laughs, He smiles... That is something new, something we have never met before.

Then you pay attention to the next: how *lonely* Judas was. Other disciples stuck together, some of them were relatives, but Judas was all alone. In addition, all the other disciples were from Galilee, but Judas was the only one from Judea. It seems to be only natural if other disciples treated him with compassion and warmth sharing their views and attitude to their common teacher Jesus. In the long run, the only persons close to Judas were them, the disciples; they were the only people with whom he spent most of the time and shared his interests; they *should* have if not understood, than *feel* Judas' loneliness, therefore they should treat him with special care and warmth... which never occurred.

Why? That time, Judas was one of them; no one could yet suspect the role he would play in the history; nobody knew or could foresee the faith of Judas Iscariot.

The common meaning existing nowadays is that the disciples were annoyed by Judas because he was mean and greedy; but what if it is not true? Did the disciples really have that negative attitude towards him? And if they did, could it be that there were some other explanations of Judas "mean" actions?

Could it be that the negative attitude to Judas from the side of other disciples, if really existed, was caused by some other reasons? For example, we know that Judas was entrusted with the common money bag. Could it be that other disciples were irritated by Judas because of the jealousy – he was new among them and got such a trust from Jesus – or, perhaps, because he did not always use the money the way *they* would like him to? You see, there is no other episode confirming Judas' greediness but the one when Mary of Bethany anointed Jesus with precious ointment of spikenard[1]. All the accusations against Judas were built on this particular episode and one phrase from one gospel,

> "This he said, not that he cared for the poor, but because he was a thief, and had the money bag and took what was put therein." *(John 12:6.)*

But it is not enough to accuse a man of theft to consider him guilty, is it? As for Judas, we'd better take into consideration that two other canonical gospels (*Mathew 26:8-9; Mark 14:4-5*) did not name the person who doubted rightness of the actions of the woman, and the third one (*Luke*) never mentioned the event. It seems logical that the words, which could be said by someone else as well, were attributed to Judas Iscariot later by the person, who was telling the story and already *had* his negative attitude towards Judas; that is why the author explained the event the way that seemed logical to him. Moreover, all the accusations and legends claiming Judas to be an assemblage of all sins were created later, *after* the tragic events took place. The events that made Judas to commit suicide and changed the name of the person into the common name.

But what if it was all a misunderstanding from the very beginning causing the negative attitude towards Judas? Could it be that all the claiming Judas legends were wrong, and people misinterpreted Judas, his reasons, and his actions in ancient times, continued to accuse him groundless during the 2000 years, and still do it? Let us try to find out the truth at least now.

Actually, there was no profit for Judas or for anybody else if the oil really was sold and the money was given to poor according to the statement; thus much is clear. Now, let us check the possibility of selling the oil and steeling the money. First, the action would be seen by all the other members of the group as the group was not numerous. Second, the stealing of money would never be accepted by the leader of the group, Jesus. That's why particularly I do not believe that these words were said by Judas: the statement was too stupid – or rather too casuistic and referred to the person doubting the honesty of Jesus' words and intentions. According to the texts, Judas never doubted Jesus.

Even if the words really belonged to Judas, there could be different reasons why he said them. For example, he could make the statement because he was a very practical man, one of those who honestly cannot understand why it is necessary to waste expensive resources if the same result can be obtained at minimal cost. If so, isn't it possible, that if Judas Iscariot lived in our times, he would have earned a fortune engaging himself in logistics? Like many other specialties, logistics requires quite a special talent, and some people possess it in a greater degree than others. Could it be that Judas Iscariot was one of those few having inborn talent to logistics, and *that* was one of the reasons why Jesus entrusted him with the common money bag?

And that is a good question indeed: why was the common money bag entrusted to Judas, to a stranger among the disciples? Sure, it was done not because Jesus was unable to understand people and relations existing between them. And definitely it wasn't done by a coincidence or because Jesus did not trust other disciples: they all lived together, ate together, and slept at the same place. One more detail: the group made together a long trip to Jerusalem, which means there *had already been* someone in the group responsible for the common money bag *before* they reached the city. There *had* to be a reason for Jesus to move the responsibility for the common money from the person, who was previously responsible for the economy of the group, to another one, to Judas. No, I do not think the decision was occasional. Jesus *had* His reasons to do it.

We continue reading of "The Gospel of Judas" and notice one more interesting thing: Judas acts not like any other disciple. Scientist who analyzed the text of "The Gospel of Judas" pointed that Judas behaved himself *as a well-bred man.* This point was neither present in any other gospel. Actually, there was never mentioned a situation allowing to say the same words about any other disciple in any other gospel. That was another thing distinguishing Judas Iscariot from all the other disciples.

According to the gospel, the only person with whom Judas communicated normally was Jesus. Besides, Jesus led long personal conversations with Judas, which we have not observed in any other gospel, except for...

The second gospel giving us the similar picture is "The Gospel According to Mary Magdalene." Here too, like in "The Gospel of Judas," we read that Jesus led long personal conversations, but in this case He talked to Mary Magdalene. Here again we read about the situations we never met in other gospels. An apocryphal "Gospel of Thomas" confirms the fact that these long talks really took place. So, what was the matter? *Why* was it like that? The science of sociology helps us to find the answer.

First, there is one thing concerning Mary Magdalene, which the researches of the ancient texts claim undoubtedly, namely, she was a well-bred person of noble origin. The second thing is that Jesus never told her the words *"Follow me."* She came to Jesus, as researchers say, voluntarily being interested in His teaching and stayed with Him[2]. The same thing did Judas Iscariot, and that is another thing they had in common.

Some apocryphal legends tell us about Judas Iscariot's origin saying that he was not just a common person. Legends tell us, he was raised by a queen of a little island together with her own son. Later, Judas joined the court of Pontius Pilate (some legends name king Herod) and soon earned the king's favour. "For his skill and beauty" Judas became responsible for the palace and for all buying [6 – 7]. The position was obviously very high and definitely required a big deal of knowledge and cleverness as well as really good manners. Judas obtained it all, which scripts and legends confirm.

By the way, here we see an indirect confirmation of our supposition of Judas' inborn talent to logistics. To be promoted like this, the person had to possess the talent indeed. Thus it becomes clear why Jesus accepted Judas "with great joy and set him in charge of all disciples" [6 – 7] and trusted him with common money. Judas was an inborn manager, you see, and apart from this he had experience in the field.

Isn't it somewhere here we find the answer to our question about the differences between gospels of Judas and of Mary Magdalene and canonical gospels? Assuming all the above said about the origin and upbringing of Jesus as true, we admit: the clue is obvious: Jesus, Judas, and Mary Magdalene belonged to the same stratum of society.

It is well-known that people from different social groups have different interests and theirs attitudes to life differ as much as their social levels. It is especially true referring to the society in which social differences were as evident as in ancient Judea.

Let us once again regard the notorious "greediness" of Judas. As we know, living in different social groups people has different habits and traditions, which can be roughly compared to the difference in the mode of living of people from neighbouring countries. The scales of their values vary too. That is why, if asked what the people consider to be necessary for living, they often name different things. For example, what is better to buy, many cheap things or a few expensive ones? Lots of vegetables or one but exotic fruit? A pack of chopped meat or one though little piece of high quality meat? A barrel of beer or a bottle of top quality vine?

There are and there can be no right or wrong answers to the questions like the above mentioned and similar to them; everything depends on people, their habits, their modes of living and their points of view. The habits and points of view are usually formed in correspondence to the social group surrounding the person. That is why any answers to the questions like above mentioned are right and wrong at the same time; everything depends on the particular person and the situation, which is typically determined by the mode of living of the person. That could be another reason for Judas "greediness": being grown up and used to live in the court circle, Judas most likely had the scale of values, which differed a lot from that of common or middle class people – the group, to which the other disciples belonged, and *that* determined his "wrong" choice when purchasing. It could easily become a source of irritation for the surrounding him members of the group who didn't shared his views and values.

Recollecting the political situation and circumstances surrounding the group, we can easily find one more reason for Judas "greediness" as well. Judas was responsible for the money of the group, no doubt about it. Then, he had to solve some problems. First, it was necessary to buy food, but there was no permanent source of income of the group members. So it was necessary to have some money "extra", though Jesus was obviously against it. On the other hand, the political situation was far from being stable; the necessity to escape and to leave the place immediately could appear any moment. Being entrusted with the common money box, it was him, Judas, who had to ensure the possibility to escape if necessary. *He* was responsible for the money and wellbeing of the group. *He* had to oversee the situation and to provide the necessary funds. *It was him, Judas Iscariot*, who had to guarantee the common wellbeing and security of all the others; *he* was responsible for the common money bag.

Now, when we get our answers, all the pieces of mosaic come to their places. Taking into consideration all the above mentioned, we see that the homogeneous group of disciples including Jesus, in fact, consisted of two coexisting together, but completely separate groups of people having significant differences between them; the difference was caused by the social origin of the participants of the groups.

The first group consisted of people "of noble origin", i.e. Jesus[3], Mary Magdalene, and Judas Iscariot. They acted like equals keeping long talks and having closer relations among themselves than between each of them and any member of the second group, which consisted of all the other disciples. The supposition is also proved by the difference in the manner of Jesus' speech, which is reflected in the texts of gospels. When communicating with Mary Magdalene and Judas Iscariot Jesus acted relaxed and allowed Himself to show His personal emotions, which is normal among friends, but which is excluded when a *teacher* talks to his pupils teaching them.

All the other disciples formed the second, i.e., the "middle-class" group. People participating in this group either belonged to middle class or were of common origin. When communicating to the second group, Jesus spoke and behaved Himself quite differently. Here, His examples were simple and easy to understand; and His philosophical constructions were direct and rational. Here, He taught, He explained, He answered the questions, while His personal attitude and relation to the people remained almost invisible.

Incidentally, it was reflected in illustrations made to the gospels: there on the pictures, Jesus was always shown as if being separated from all the other participants of the action. This is the typical situation I mentioned at the very beginning of the book, i.e., "a teacher in the classroom". The texts of gospels, read by artists, acted on their subconscious and that's why they created the compositions this way. It was simply impossible to compose the picture differently; not after reading the canonical gospels.

The impression is quite different when we read "The Gospel of Judas" and "The Gospel According to Mary Magdalene". Here, Jesus *teaches* but not only. Here, Jesus *shares* His knowledge, His visions, His thoughts… These three persons communicated as equals, *as friends*; Jesus talked not only *to* those two but *with* them.

These three spoke the same language; they understood each other much better than all other disciples or pupils of Jesus understood Him. There was a difference in the way Jesus communicated with Mary Magdalene and Judas and all the others in His group; and that was the source of the indignity and rejection felt by members of the second group towards Judas Iscariot. Here from raised jealousy mixed with the social disparity and cultural difference.

Actually, there was one thing more, one more reason and the aspect of the problem, and we are going to learn about it in the next chapter.

Notes

1. Mathew 26:6-13; Mark 14:3-8; John 12:1-8

2. Could it be that she simply fell in love with Jesus? Women used to share the ideas of those they love, you know.

3. By the way, reading attentively the canonical gospels, we find the confirmation that Jesus Himself knew He was a king even there. That is why Jesus neither denied nor confirmed it, and we read,

    > "And it came to pass, when Jesus had ended these sayings, the people were astonished at His doctrine; for He taught them as one having authority and not as the scribes" *(Mathew 7:28-29).*

That is why Jesus underlines distance between Him and disciples as:

> "The disciple is not above his master, nor the servant above his lord. It is enough for the disciple that he be as his master, and the servant as his lord." *(Mathew 10:24-25)*;

> "Remember the word that I said unto you: 'The servant is not greater than his lord.' If they have persecuted Me, they will also persecute you; if they have kept My saying, they will keep yours also." *(John 15:20)*,

and some other places. Was it, maybe, an open secret, i.e., certain people knew about it, although one might expect it to be a secret?

And there is one thing more. You see, *a teacher* is always *happy* if his pupil goes further than the teacher, but *a king* would never accept the situation when a servant becomes greater than the lord.

11

Peter

Although there were all in all twelve disciples who became famous, we know not equally much about every one of them. Some of the disciples were, so to say, more visible than the others and we know a bit more about those few. For example, we know that Mathew (Levi) was a toll collector; we know that James and John were sons of Zebedee who had possibility to hire servants, but still had to work himself; and we definitely know much more about Peter (Simon).

As for the last one, we know his real name - Simon, sometimes occurring in the form Symeon *(Acts 15:14; 2 Peter 1:1)*; we know that when Jesus called him, he was fishing together with his brother Andrew; and we know that he was the son of Jona (Johannes) and was born in Bethsaida, a town on Lake Genesareth in Galilee *(John 1:42, 44)*. But is it true that Peter (Simon) was *only* a fisherman?

The first thing that was not said, but can be guessed is that Simon (Peter) was the elder brother, and Andrew was the younger one. That is why every time they are mentioned together, their names are given in this order: first Simon (Peter) and then Andrew. Senior, being more important, goes first. In addition, it is known that to the moment of their meeting with Jesus, Simon (Peter) had already been married. It is also mentioned in the gospels, that Simon (Peter) had his own family, and Andrew lived together with them, and so did Simon's mother-in-low (*Mark 1:29-31; Luke 4:38-39*).

Second. Professional fishermen catch fish not only for the sake of pleasure or to satisfy the needs of their own families. After the fish is caught, it is necessary to do something with the catch; i.e., it must be *sold*. This moment is very important for our story. Now, let us think about it.

In general, there are two principal ways to sell things: wholesale and retail. Fishermen, usually, never engage themselves in retail. They typically sell the catch to wholesalers who further continue to deal with it.

Who could possibly be responsible for selling the catch and for all the negotiations with merchants? It is clear: the responsibility belonged to the eldest man, i.e., to the head of the family.

Unlike the case with the sons of Zebedee, James and John, the father of Simon (Peter) and Andrew was never mentioned. Thus we make a conclusion, that either their father was dead, or they lived separately and had business of their own, which is more likely. Consequently, it was Simon (Peter) who was the head of the family and had responsibility for the trade and all the financial negotiations.

Could it be that the brothers engaged themselves in retail too and, perhaps, had a shop of their own in the nearest town? No one can say it for sure; but this possibility can't be excluded. Anyway, we can be absolutely sure that the element of successful trade was of great importance in the lives of the brothers. It was not so much a good catch, but *a good sale* of the catch that brought profit and prosperity to the family.

You can see now, how important the element of the successful trade was in their lives. And the significant role in the business belonged to Simon (Peter) *as he was the head of the family.* The wellbeing of his own family, the wellbeing of his brother and his mother-in-low (were there, perhaps, some other members of the family though never mentioned?) depended on the Simon's ability to trade and to negotiate. Simon (Peter) *had* to have the mentality of a merchant; it was *his* responsibility, and it was his obligation. Actually, I think he was an inborn merchant exactly the same way, as Judas Iscariot was an inborn manager.

And now I explain why I mean it to be so important. You see, many things can be changed in a person when the one is under hypnotic suggestion. A hypnotizer can make the person to forget unforgettable or to recollect something that never happened. But the main characteristics, *the way the person thinks* remains unchanged – if the task of the hypnotizer is not to influence this particularly part of the personality; and even if so, it's rather doubtful that they succeed in it.

But Jesus never meant changing the personalities. After 2000 years we hear His words, *"Follow Me!"* That was all, nothing more was said, *no other task was given.* There was absolutely nothing regarding possible changing of personal features. The people following Jesus *remained themselves in everything* considering their personal features, but one thing: they followed Jesus everywhere, as if being chained to Him. After His words, they became His permanent companions and pupils, they became the disciples.

Still, no matter that they followed Jesus permanently and never thought of possibility to leave Him, they often doubted Jesus and His teaching, which we read in gospels, and with which Jesus reproached them several times[1]. By the way, it also proves that the personalities were not changed as a result of the suggestion: Jesus ordered them *to follow* Him, not *to believe* Him and His doctrine; He did not *persuade*, but *taught* them.

Simon (Peter) kept his mentality of a merchant too, which means that his way of thinking was really special. To be successful in any profession, a person needs *to think properly*, you know.

The action of Jesus, when He entrusted the common economy of the group and the money bag to Judas, but not to Peter, inevitably hurt the last much. Peter meant, he had an experience in the field; he meant himself to be a clever and responsible person – and perhaps he was like that indeed. Besides, Peter was deeply devoted to Jesus, which nobody doubts. But Jesus still preferred Judas for the task. Thus Peter could not help feeling himself offended and got a negative attitude towards Judas – especially if Judas was younger and belonged to another generation, which some researchers claim.

In the long run, Peter's feelings are easy to understand; just put yourself into his shoes. He was a mature person having some (if not many) years of experience of successful trading and negotiations on behalf of his large family; he used to provide its wellbeing. He *knew* how to use the money properly. He loved Jesus with all his heart; but all of a sudden, Jesus entrusted all the financial activity and recourses to an absolute upstart, to a stranger among the disciples. He, Peter, was together with Jesus from the very beginning, but Judas joined the company much later. Judas was the one who behaved himself weird, and it was absolutely not clear what could be expected from him. It is obvious that Peter could not help feeling irritation and jealousy towards Judas. Doesn't the history conveys to us the echo of these feelings?..

And now, let us postpone the story for a while and, despite the couple of thousand years that passed, try to find out what kind of person Peter really was.

Everything positive about him we already know; the Church carefully saved it in the scripts, traditions and canons. Peter's name opens the list of the twelve elected; it is about him Jesus said, "thou art Peter, and upon this rock I will build My church; and the gates of hell shall not prevail against it" *(Mathew 16:18)*;

to him Jesus gave keys of the Kingdom of Heaven; to him Jesus said,

"Feed My sheep." *(John 21:16)*

According to canonical gospels, Peter declares his devotion to Jesus many times. However during the Last Supper, Jesus casually predicts Peter's threefold repudiation *(Mathew 26:34; Mark 14:30; Luke 22:34; John 13:38)*.

After the resurrection, Jesus showed Himself to His pupils. He asked Peter tree times if Peter loved Him; and after Peter had answered thrice affirmative, He named Peter to be the first among disciples *(John 21:14-17)*. The thrice repeated assurances in devotion removed the triple repudiation of Peter – at least, that was the explanation we got. Then, Peter acted as a leader of the Twelve in the election of a replacement for Judas Iscariot and in the public declaration at Pentecost *(Acts 1.12-26; 2:14-40)* – he was definitely a charismatic leader. At the same time, Peter began his preaching, performed many miracles, and in the end voluntarily returned to Rome accepting his martyrdom on the cross. Later, the institution of Pope was established denouncing the Bishop of Rome as successor of St. Peter, the chief pastor of the whole Church, and the Vicar of Christ upon earth.

And what apocryphal texts would tell us in addition to all that? Maybe, we'll find something significant there? Indeed, not all of the scripts are as addicted to exaggeration and wonder as they are claimed to be.

"Gospel of Thomas" does not remind "The Gospel According to Mary Magdalene". The two gospels are dated from about the same time; the former is dated to the middle of the first century, and the letter – to the beginning of the second century. Nevertheless, their languages are totally different and they consider entirely different things, though… There is an episode in "The Gospel of Thomas"… And the similar episode is described in "The Gospel According to Mary Magdalene" even more detailed… But I'd better quote them both here.

"Gospel of Thomas":

> "114. Simon Peter said to them, "Make Mary leave us, for females don't deserve life."
>
> Jesus said, "Look, I will guide her to make her male, so that she too may become a living spirit resembling you males. For every female who makes herself male will enter the kingdom of Heaven."

"Gospel according to Mary Magdalene", Chapter 9:

> "1) When Mary had said this, she fell silent, since it was to this point that the Savior had spoken with her.
>
> 2) But Andrew answered and said to the brethren, Say what you wish to say about what she has said. I at least do not believe that the Savior said this. For certainly these teachings are strange ideas.
>
> 3) Peter answered and spoke concerning these same things.
>
> 4) He questioned them about the Savior: Did He really speak privately with a woman and not openly to us? Are we to turn about and all listen to her? Did He prefer her to us?

5) Then Mary wept and said to Peter, My brother Peter, what do you think? Do you think that I have thought this up myself in my heart, or that I am lying about the Savior?

6) Levi answered and said to Peter, Peter you have always been hot tempered.

7) Now I see you contending against the woman like the adversaries.

8) But if the Savior made her worthy, who are you indeed to reject her? Surely the Savior knows her very well.

9) That is why He loved her more than us. Rather let us be ashamed and put on the perfect Man, and separate as He commanded us and preach the gospel, not laying down any other rule or other law beyond what the Savior said."

Don't you think that in both cases there happened exactly the same thing, namely, Peter confronted Mary Magdalene; and he did it by the *only one* reason, because she was *a woman*? More than that, the words in the quotes sound in such a way, that it becomes clear: the arguing was not something either occasional or happening for the first time. It is obvious, other disciples were much more tolerant with Mary Magdalene than Peter, and they even criticized him for his enmity.

As for Jesus, the situation looks quite different. If we take into consideration all His actions, words and statements regarding women, it turns out that Jesus, in fact, was, perhaps, one of the first fighters for women's rights, for their education, and their equal with men's place in the society.

But what about Peter? In addition to the quoted texts there are some other texts confirming Peter's negative attitude to women. First of all, I can mention in this connection apocryphal scripts "Acts of Peter" and later apocrypha telling, first of all, about the martyrdom of Peter. According to the scripts, with his preaching, among other things, Peter inspired women with disgust to marriage and "sinful life". As a result, he incurred anger and hatred of Roman authorities and imposed persecutions.

It is puzzling, isn't it, what did women do wrong to him?

And now let us tell the situation one more time, but let's do it using contemporary language; and let us try to forget all about the names of the characters.

In the most general terms the situation is as following: a man hates women considering them to be worthless and useless creatures; and their sexuality is particularly disgusting for him. At the same time, the same man to the end of his days, until death, loves a man and astonish the surrounding him people with the level of his devotion to the person. At the same time, this very man hates one woman *especially*; and this woman presumably has close, personal relations with the man, he himself is devoted to. His negative attitude towards this woman is so strong, that even puzzles their common friends / acquaintances, who are really displeased with such his behaviour. Moreover, a good and friendly attitude of the man, he is devoted to, to another man causes the sharp negative emotions towards the last one.

Do you recognise the situation? Can you guess the reason why it all happened? Shall I give you the names or you call them yourselves?

Yes, I think, Peter was homosexual, although he himself, probably, never even suspected it. It happens sometimes, you know. His passion to Jesus was so fiery and immeasurable (which did not, though, prevent him from renouncing Jesus), that their contemporaries were amazed. Peter even voluntarily came to his martyrdom returning to

Rome and required to be crucified his head down saying he could not afford thoughts of equality with Jesus even in his death.

Unrealized sexuality that expressed itself in religious fanaticism… It was neither the first, nor the last case in the history of humankind.

True love that would deserve admiration, if not for the consequences it entailed for all of us.

As for the consequences – I'll tell you about them at the very end of the book, in the Inference.

Notes

1.   Mathew 6:30, 8:26, 14:31, 16:8; Luke 12:28

12

How It Was

And now, if you admit the possibility of the things I told you above, I tell you what really happened that distant spring in Jerusalem, when there were laid basis to the fundamental features of our contemporary world and the Christianity in the form we know today.

1

I accept as true, that the philosophy and the views of Jesus Christ were formed as a result of His dreams and visions which were caused by His extrasensory perception and the disturbance of the System. The dreams and visions were source of His ideas, and to some extent they were inducement of His actions. You see, I really consider Jesus to be a God-Man – to a certain degree though. With that I mean, that He was able to "read" the information performed by the System and could use the tremendous spiritual force He possessed. What was even more important – and I want to underline it once again – He was a really special person having incredibly positive attitude towards people and to the world. Jesus was brought up as a king though having necessity to hide Himself. He had a deep understanding of His place in the world and possessed an extremely strong feeling of responsibility.

Frightened by the dreams and visions showing Him horrible future, which would expect people and the world if nothing was changed, Jesus left the normal life He led before, became baptized, and began His way to Calvary. Trying to save the world and His people, Jesus began to preach a new, more humane belief. It was the only way He saw to avoid the inevitable and to change the future. He told His visions to people and, first of all, to the disciples as the reality to come, as something He knew and meant to be true. That time, Jesus began to flaunt all the abilities He hid previously, and first of all His ability to heal, as a proof of being the son of God, which He saw in the vision under the rite of baptism, and which He absolutely believed Himself meaning His spiritual rebirth.

Jesus left the place where He had lived with the family, saying with bitterness,

> "A prophet is not without honor, save in his own country
> and in his own house," *(Mathew 13:57).*

On His way to Jerusalem, Jesus recruited some people and made them to become His disciples. Probably He did it obeying His dreams too, we know nothing about it; no place was mentioned why Jesus chose particularly these people[1]. On the other hand, it was only natural: whom could Jesus possibly tell about it that time? He could share His personal thoughts only with someone who would fully understand Him, someone close to Him; but at that very moment, there were no such people around Him yet.

Jesus rejects His previous life and, perhaps, all the habits He had before and completely devotes Himself to *only one* aim: *He teaches.* It seems like He is in a great hurry, as if something urges Him on. This "something" is the information He receives from the System and its increasing pressure.

Jesus gives no rest either to Himself, or to disciples who accompanied Him permanently. Now, all His life and all His talks are circulating about one item: His doctrine, in which Jesus believes Himself, and which He means to be obliged to explain to as many people as it is only possible. That makes Him to tell so many stories explaining and depicting His ideas.

2

And Jesus performs healings. He makes it with one touch, with one glance... It looks as if it does not demand any effort from Him, but only a person, who could at least once help another one in this way, can understand how much efforts the process takes and how exhausting this activity is.

Jesus works to complete exhaustion spurred by His visions: those He can't help talking about, and those we know nothing about yet, or those – who knows! – He never runs a risk to tell anyone, or they were not found yet. Maybe we'll find some more scripts and learn more about His visions, thoughts, and ideas, but maybe He did not tell more just because there was no one closed enough to Him at the time? There were simply no such people in His surrounding to whom Jesus could trust with His deepest thoughts; with whom He could share His feelings; the one who could ease His burden: responsibility for the future of His people and the world.

Strictly speaking, *that* was Jesus' way to the Calvary, to which He went, carrying on His shoulders the heavy Cross: the pressure of the System demanding changes in the society; knowledge, He was unable to understand Himself, neither to explain it to others; the reason for Him to be crucified. He was bearing it, like in some time later He would bear the wooden cross, on which He would be crucified ending His days in martyrdom.

During all this time, Jesus speaks of blood and of approaching tragedies that plagued Him in His visions and had to be prevented. How? – By abandoning the old teachings arousing aggression in people no matter how "true" and reasonable the principles of these teachings seemed to be and by accepting the new teaching, which was much more humane. The church itself, according to the new teaching, should be concentrated not on the external attributes, but on the inner content giving people hope and promising reward for the good actions.

The researchers claim: that time and that place there was a lot of preachers declaring similar views and beliefs. All of them ended their lives the same way: they were killed; most of them were crucified. That was the sign of the times.

3

Luckily, all of a sudden there came help to Jesus: Judas Iscariot and later Mary of Magdala joined the group. They were people belonging to the same stratum of society as Jesus. Then the life seemed to be a little bit easier for Him; then Jesus obtained friends with whom He could talk.

Of course, confidence did not come immediately; and establishing of friendly relations demanded time. Nevertheless, it happened, and Jesus got moral support. That time, He had people with whom He could relief His soul and share His deepest thoughts and feelings.

It is interesting though that we can't find stories about the things, which made Jesus to *rush* either in "The Gospel of Judas" or in "The Gospel According to Mary Magdalene" or any other script. But except for *words,* there are *actions,* and they speak for themselves.

4

Things are coming to a head – Jesus begins to see His *special* dreams again. Only this time they head Him to the death. Somehow they are similar to those that made Him to change His life, but that time Jesus searched rescuing from the horror of Satan, and now it is God to push Him.

Obviously, these dreams came to Him not once. "Just dreams" can come and go, but a person being under the presser of the System experiences things differently. These visions do not leave, they come time after time, they stay, they press, and they demand actions. What did He see?..

Jesus is exhausted; He is completely squeezed out; He is in despair. The story shows us His state: there in garden of Gethsemane Jesus prays for mercy. – No answer... Jesus understands that the inevitable *is* unavoidable. Now, He can no longer either think or talk about anything else, but that horror, which is waiting for Him, that He must pass through.

It is now, we seem to have a choice. We are smart, we know a lot... and still there are fanatics living among us today, beaching themselves to deep wounds and voluntarily crucifying themselves for Christ. Is it *that* He taught people?.. So, how could we expect Him not to fulfil the actions, which He meant to be required by God?

Jesus can't help talking about His visions; He talks about them almost with everybody. He shares His *deepest* thoughts with His close people, friends: with Judas Iscariot and Mary Magdalene. Only with them could He share such ideas of His.

Echoes of those conversations convey to us through "The Gospel of Judas" and "The Gospel According to Mary Magdalene". Only echoes, without something very important, that Jesus obviously asked not to tell anyone... Why did He do it? – I don't know, probably because He did not utterly believed it Himself?..

5

There comes the last night – the Last Supper. Jesus' nerves are stretched to the limit – no longer is He able to withstand the stress. Whatever should happen – let it happen fast, *NOW*. Jesus sends Judas Iscariot for the treason. And there is only one thing He asks Judas for,

"What thou doest, do quickly," *(John 13:27)*.

Jesus does not hide the fact that He sends Judas to authorities to extradite Him. He is tired too much and can neither think nor talk about anything else, except for the awful future that expects Him: the martyrdom He must go through. It is here, He mentions as-a-matter-of-fact about Peter's threefold renunciation – in spite of all the assurances of love and devotion, at a moment of danger Peter will deny Him.

And everything happened as predicted. Judas went to the authorities and volunteered to indicate Jesus giving them the proposal they gladly accepted. For the betrayal, Judas was being paid and he throws the money off: he did it not for the money's sake. He acts moved by his devotion to The-One-Who-Sent-him and by his trust in Him and His ideas. Although, judging by how long Jesus encouraged him to do it, Judas' doubts were significant.

Judas with the officers comes to the previously agreed place of meeting with Jesus, in Gethsemane garden. There Jesus is waiting for the arrest "resting" together with His disciples. When the guards approach, Jesus wakes up the disciples and together with them goes to meet the newcomers.

Why did Jesus wake up disciples? – Because of one reason: *He needed witnesses*. He knew what should happen, He believed in it, and He needed people to confirm that it would be Him, Jesus – there, up on the cross...

And once again Jesus urges Judas.

Judas comes to Jesus, embraces Him and gives Him the last kiss: he says farewell to his beloved friend and teacher[2]. Judas knows about the excruciating death which expects Jesus; he also knows that Jesus believes it to be the only way to fulfil the prediction. The prediction, He made Himself...

6

Jesus was led away. Heated crowd started hunting for His followers; and Peter, exactly according to the prediction of Jesus, renounced Him thrice.

It is just amazing, how people acted that moment! Even if we assume that only one fifth of all the stories, told about Jesus, was true, people should have spoken in His defence, which, however, never happened. The same people, who yesterday listened to Jesus and, perhaps, admired Him being healed by Him, are now howling, "*Crucify him!*"

That is exactly the mode of human mass behaviour described in works of Professor A.L. Chizhevsky,

> "Researcher... is being amazed by astonishing ability of a human been to become involved into a crazy whirlpool of psychopathological epidemics. The one, who only yesterday harshly denounced one or another mass movement, becomes its follower and its victim today. Mental infection shows itself quickly and decisively, covering with a speed of lightning huge circles of population," *[8]*.

All this happens under the influence of extremely high activity of the Sun.

By the way, I think if historians use results achieved by researches of solar activity they will be able to determine the year of the events with high accuracy.

7

The execution. Jesus has been crucified. And here, I think, the most important things begin to happen:

> "about the ninth hour Jesus cried out with a loud voice, saying, "Eli, Eli, lama sabachthani?" that is to say, "My God, My God, why hast Thou forsaken Me?" *(Mathew 27:46)*

You see, Jesus knew perfectly well what He had to go through. He was neither the first, nor the only one person preaching alternative belief that time. Neither He was a fool – sorry for the rude word. He knew His death would be long and painful, but *it was not the thing He spoke about.* It seems as if He was expecting something that *should* happen, but didn't occur.

He was waiting for the promised miracle. The miracle He saw in His vision, which should happen to prove the truthfulness of His teaching. The miracle that should change the future of the world, the main purpose of His existence, in the name of which He did everything leaving His former live forever.

But we live in the real world, which is bent to physical laws. Miracle did not happen. Jesus died crucified.

8

The Gospel of Judas ends at the arrest of Jesus.

Other gospels tell us, that Judas committed suicide. According to the evangelists, he hanged himself not being able to bear his penitence.

It would have been nice if all traitors guilty in death of innocent people acted like this. Life, however, shows us quite a different pattern of behaviour of the people who deliberately commit betrayal.

Shall we, maybe, admit that Judas' moral standards were as high as he could not stand the conflict with himself? Then the version of "the dirty traitor" does not work at all: having so high moral standards Judas wouldn't be able to commit betrayal.

Let us ask ourselves; in which case, in general, does a person commit a suicide? Well, as psychologists claim, a person can do it, first, trying to attract attention to him-/herself with the hope to be saved in time (strongly doubtful that this situation is suitable for our case); and second, when the person sees no future for him-/herself, can't find any way out of the situation, and is not able to see anything good in the future. The whole world falls collapsing around the person, and there is no place in it for the one.

That's it! That situation looks exactly like our case! You see, to make Judas to extradite Him to the authorities, Jesus *had* to tell him the reason why He considered it necessary to be done. More than that, He had to *persuade* Judas to do it; to *convince* him that *there would be* a miracle, *the* miracle.

During the execution, Judas, just like Jesus, was excruciatingly waiting for *a miracle*. The miracle, which was promised and predicted by Jesus; the miracle that never happened: Jesus died on the cross.

And then, the whole world collapsed for Judas. Everything he trusted, everything preached by Jesus proved false. *The miracle had never happened. Of all the things they trusted in and devoted their lives to, nothing happened, nothing was real. Worse, it appeared that he indeed betrayed his dear friend and teacher and condemn Him to the horrible death.*

No wonder Judas committed suicide; who is strong enough to stand such thoughts and feelings?..

Being absolutely desperate after that what happened, or, better to say, what did *not* happen, Judas condemned himself to the worst punishment possible: he would hang himself on a tree. According to the archaic tradition, with doing it he became cursed by God (*Deuteronomy 21:22-23*).

9

Friday. The burial of Jesus. For the burial, His body is delivered to Joseph of Arimathea at his request. Joseph of Arimathea prepares the body to the burial. According to the Jewish tradition, he wraps Jesus' body in a clean linen cloth with spices

> "and laid it in his own new tomb, which he had hewn
> out in the rock. And he rolled a great stone to the door
> of the sepulcher and departed," *(Mathew 27:60)*.

Everything is correct: according to Jewish tradition, the deceased must be buried on the day of the death, i.e., during the first 24 hours.

Then, Saturday comes. According to the sacred tradition of Sabbath, nobody works that day. The tradition is highly respected and strictly kept among Jews even now.

Sunday. Mary Magdalene (perhaps with some women) comes to the Jesus' tomb bringing some sweet spices (fragrances) to anoint His body.

WHAT?!!! WHAT ARE THEY TALKING ABOUT?!!! Such action is not possible in general either then or nowadays! It can't be classified anything else but abuse!

Just think: the person is dead and buried, and his tomb is closed. And after that, and after the second day has passed, someone is going to open the tomb again?!! Well, in the Middle Ages, people were burnt on fire for smaller crimes.

The strictly negative attitude against the opening of graves still exists and is deemed as absolutely unacceptable having the name DESECRATION OF GRAVES. The action could be possibly done only by a person who had really serious reasons to do it – and definitely without any witnesses present. But in our story, there were *women* intending to commit the action; in addition, they were *good women* as it is known they kept Sabbath!..

No, I don' think it was possible. It is strongly doubtful that anointment of Jesus' body was the real motive of Mary's visit to His tomb. Rather, this excuse was invented especially *to explain* the visit, and it is most probable that it was done much later, when the legend of His resurrection has already existed, as well as the legend about His appearance to Mary Magdalene, to Peter, to disciples, and to people believing in Him.

10
The second version; what *I* mean to happen.

There was a third person knowing that during the crucifixion *the miracle* should take place. That was Mary Magdalene, the third person standing apart from all the disciples, but the second if not the first one close to Jesus.

Mary was a woman, and she reached for knowledge. Jesus, on the other hand, respected and encouraged this interest in women. His soft and tolerant attitude towards women is obvious to everyone who read gospels.

Apart from being a woman, Mary Magdalene was His friend and a person speaking the same language with Jesus as much as it was only possible. That's why Jesus couldn't help sharing His thoughts, feelings, doubts, and expectations with her exactly the same way, as He could not help telling the things He was concerned about to Judas.

Everybody needs to share the thoughts and feelings and to relieve the mind from time to time, especially if the person is under permanent stress as it was with Jesus. When the time of the crucifixion became closer, He could not help talking about it with her too, but in this case He had *to think* before talking. There were things He told everyone; and there were things He definitely did not tell everyone. Those things He could share only with His bosom friends. But in the first case, when Jesus spoke to Judas, He talked to make Judas to extradite Him as He Himself could not go to the authorities begging for the arrest and crucifixion; there are rules in every game, you know.

In the second case, i.e., speaking to Mary Magdalene, Jesus talked simply because she was *a woman*. He couldn't allow Himself to cause her such pain; He had *to prepare* her for the event: He was a man of humane character indeed feeling pain of a nearby person as His own. Besides, it was necessary to protect her against some stupidities she obviously would do during His future arrest and execution, which could harm her. Women often act irrational; they are much more influenced by their emotions than men, and they are not easy to control themselves...

Jesus was arrested and crucified. Mary Magdalene was waiting for the miracle that never occurred. Still, unlike Judas, she did not commit a suicide. Why not?..

No doubt, she believed Jesus, and when the promised miracle did not happen, the world around her collapsed exactly the same way, as it did for Judas, or even worse as she was a woman and Jesus was the man she loved. She loved Him – because she could not help doing it; because He was the person He was: the best man among all; and because He was her teacher to whom she volunteered to come. She came – and stayed with Him. So, why didn't she commit a suicide too, when Jesus died?

I do not think Jesus meant less to her than to Judas. I do not think she loved Jesus less than Peter. I do not think she was a woman without emotions. I think she was a woman of clever mind and strong personality. Only by that we can explain why that time, when it was unacceptable for a woman to stay alone without either a husband or male relatives around her – if she was not a whore, of course, and Mary Magdalene definitely was not the one – she stayed with Jesus becoming one of His disciples. The only one woman among men…

I do not think she was Jesus' wife. If it was so, it would most probably be mentioned in one of the scripts. Neither do I think she was His secret wife. There was absolutely no reason to keep the marriage in secrecy if any. They were adults, and it would be only natural if they were married[3]. Besides, Jesus was never against institution of marriage. He was against *amorality*, debauchery, and, possibly, prostitution, but not against family relations. Historians claim that His disciples had families and wives. You see, *it was only normal* to be married and to have family… And yet, Jesus was not married.

Jesus simply had not enough time to marry Mary Magdalene. He had neither enough time, nor moral strength to get married or even think about family life: the pressure of the System was too hard. Apart of this, He knew He was to die; so, how could He run a risk to take responsibility for a woman, especially for the one He loved? He was all in His work and His task… which is typical for men.

And there is one thing more. There exists the only thing in the world, that would prevent a woman in Mary's situation from committing a suicide, that would keep her alive no matter what happens around her, and that would give her strength to do whatever she means necessary to be done. All the things fell into their places if we admit that Mary was pregnant with a baby of the man she loved, of Jesus.

We all are living souls. We all feel and react. We all have hormones influencing our behaviour. Being under stress, we all try to find salvation in the one we love. And when we have it *really bad*, we pay absolutely no attention to any conventions, as, e.g., what the documents and traditions dictate. We just clasp to the bosom of the one we love and hide ourselves in him from all the troubles of the world. Or in *her*.

Jesus was not inclined to homosexuality; otherwise His attitude towards women would be different. And Mary Magdalene was close to Him, and she loved Him. It would be strange and unnatural if the things happened differently.

But believe me; a woman, bearing a child of the man she loves, is able to perform many things indeed.

11
So, Jesus has died, and Mary Magdalene knows that the miracle He predicted did not happen. Everything was in vain. *Was everything in vain? Did Jesus die for nothing?!!* No! There will never be this way!

Mary Magdalene decides to make the miracle, expected and predicted by Jesus, with her own hands.

I can't prove it all really happened this way, and the things were as described below. I write what *I* would do, if I were in her shoes.

Mary Magdalene hires people, most likely tramps or homeless, who would not tell anybody – just because no one would listen to them – to remove the rock from the sepulchre, to take the body and to rebury Jesus in some other place, which she, probably, pointed to them.

Why these people had to be tramps or homeless? – First, because they usually work for small money and as long as they are paid they do not care about any rules and traditions; and second... You see, Jesus was known that time, but He was not so much famous among His contemporaries as everybody would know His face and His story. It was only later, He became *thus* famous. On the other hand, crucifixion was quite an ordinary execution those days. Hence the second reason is, these people just would not know, who the man was and what it all was about; and even if knowing they were absolutely indifferent to it.

It is as well possible that it was not several people, but just one man having the same reasons as above mentioned: he agreed to make the job, whatever the reason was, and to get paid for it. Not everybody is interested in politics, you know. Actually, I can easier imagine Mary Magdalene talking to one decent man than to a band of tramps.

Most likely, Mary Magdalene paid them – or him – with the money she took from the common money bag. They were really close those three: Jesus, Mary Magdalene, and Judas. Judas definitely trusted Mary Magdalene, and most likely, the money bag was left some place, which was not available to everybody, but easily accessible to her. Is it here, perhaps, we find the reason for appearance of the legend of Judas being a thief – the money bag disappeared without a trace, thus he, probably, stole it.

Obviously, these people (or that man, whoever they or he was) had to do the job on Saturday, which is doubtful because of the Sabbath tradition, or on Sunday morning, which is much more likely. In this case, it is clear why Mary Magdalene went to the tomb all alone leaving the women behind her – if she really came with them, which I definitely believe as it is much easier to a woman to go with some other women or at least with one person of the same sex especially if it considers some important things to happen, than to do it alone. In our case, it was something *very* important; but before coming with the women to sepulchre, Mary Magdalene had to check if everything had been done properly and is ready for them to see. If not, she would find a reason to make the women to come back later.

They (or he) managed to do everything in time. Mary Magdalene paid them (or him) and they (or he) left the place. Being afraid that some of the women could see her talking to a stranger, Mary Magdalene invented the story about the gardener:

> "…she turned around and saw Jesus standing, and knew not that it was Jesus.
>
> Jesus said unto her, "Woman, why weepest thou? Whom seekest thou?" She, supposing Him to be the gardener, said unto Him, "Sir, if thou have borne Him hence, tell me where thou hast laid Him, and I will take Him away." *(John 20:14-15)*

The explanation was made and later on it found its place in the history.

Anyway, if, basing on this version, I would search for Jesus' grave, I would do it somewhere within a half an hour walk distance from the place of His first burial; otherwise these people (or this person) would not manage to do the job in time: as the history tells us, the visitors came early in the morning.

And then Mary Magdalene tells the women the legend of the resurrection. Angel (or Jesus Christ Himself) appeared in front of her told her that the resurrection happened indeed. Mary is shaken, accompanying her women exclaim "ah!", "oh!" and clasp their hands in astonishment.

Pay attention to the following: it was *only* Mary Magdalene who saw the Angel(s) or Jesus Christ who gave her the message about the Resurrection, *not any other* women were present at a time.

Then, they all return to the place they lived and tell the story of Jesus' resurrection to the disciples[4].

And now it is Peters' turn to step forward. You do remember, don't you: he had a quick mind of a merchant. Possessing this he had to be able to found soon his feet in a new surrounding and make the most profitable /advantageous for him solution.

Peter loves Jesus, no matter He is dead. Of all the rivals there remained only Mary Magdalene. And yet Peter has pangs of conscience caused by his triple denying of Jesus; he did it exactly as predicted.

Peter grasps the idea. Soon after, he declares: Jesus showed Himself to him too and talked to him. More than that, Jesus *only showed* Himself to Mary, but He *talked* to Peter: He asked him trice if he, Peter, loves Him, Jesus, and after Peter tree times confirmed that *he really, indeed* loves Him – of course, Peter did love Jesus! – Jesus forgave Peter for his threefold repudiation and told him that he is and will remain *the first* among disciples (*John 21:14-17*).

Who of all the Jesus' pupils would doubt the omnipotence of Savoir, if He Himself was preparing them for such turn of the events, and there had already been two people claiming themselves to be eyewitness of His resurrection? Besides, there was no Jesus' body in the sepulchre; it had disappeared indeed leaving all the clothes He was buried in...

12

And people began to see miraculous appearances of Christ. He was seen by His disciples, by bystanders, by occasional people, and by people who just heard about Him. Some people invented the stories, some saw Him in reality.

> "Mental infection shows itself quickly and decisively, covering with a speed of lightning huge circles of population,"

wrote Professor A. L. Chizhevsky [8] of the phenomena that not once occurred in the history of humankind.

13

And now we move forward to the next mystery. We know perfectly well, what Peter and other disciples did after the Jesus' death; but what about Mary Magdalene? She completely disappeared from the stage of the history. Nobody knows anything about her. It seems as if she simply vanished into thin air.

Maybe she really did it? Actually, she could really do it on purpose: Mary Magdalene knew perfectly well the nature of Peter and his attitude towards her, as well as the fact that he definitely knew the true value of her (and his own) words of miraculous appearances of Jesus. Taking into consideration that she was pregnant (without being married, by the way)… Actually, in this case, there was really only possible way out for her: to escape, which she, apparently, did.

If Mary Magdalene continued to stay among people, who were witnesses to the whole story, having the baby growing in her womb, most likely, she would be proclaimed a whore (as it was, actually, done centuries later anyway), and not a single story about holiness of Jesus Christ would withstand the pressure of public opinion reinforced by rumours. Such development of the events, first, could not be allowed by Mary Magdalene herself, and second, it would never be allowed by Peter, which she apparently knew. Thus she disappeared to begin a new life at a new place. The money for the journey was obviously taken from the common money bag. It was not a stealing – it was the measure to save Jesus' child.

14

Option Two. The Angels appear on the stage again.

According to the gospels[5], it was an Angel(s) waiting for Mary Magdalene at Jesus' tomb. It was the Angel to give her the news about His resurrection. There were Angels proclaiming that some day He would come back.

Let us try to see what we get if we accept the assumption of the existence of the organization, which we discusses in the previous chapters and agreed to call Angels of Rescue and Protection, Guarding Angels, or Angels of God.

Angels, i.e., members of the secret society guarding treasures of Jewish kings and protecting the royal family, were rather displeased with the activity of Jesus. If He tried to unite people, to organise the resistance, which could result in liberation of the country and restoring of the kingdom, it would be understandable. In this case, they would definitely give Him support including financial one. But His activity as a healer and a preacher could not be useful to the people of Israel; thus Angels could not possibly have a wish to support Jesus. Jewish people could expect nothing but troubles from such a king, if He would be openly proclaimed the one. There was no wonder about healing abilities of Jesus; His ancestors were famous because of them. As for His clairvoyant talent, if it helped to return the state and independence to Jewish people, it would be invaluable. But it was not necessary to be a clairvoyant to understand, that Jewish people could expect nothing good under Roman domination over the region. Jesus' preaching of a new belief could result only in exacerbating of the plight of Jewish people and entail further repressions. The decision was made, and Angels disappeared from life of Jesus.

Did He ever know of their existence? Most likely, not. If He was the person they were waiting for to proclaim as the King, they would probably show themselves. But as Jesus, even as a child, showed Himself to be *strange,* they remained in the shadows.

Still Angels never ceased watching His activity. They stopped to give Jesus financial support, which they occasionally provided earlier by supporting His parents[6]. It is clearly illustrated by the following: during all the journeys of Mary and Joseph, as well as during Jesus' childhood, we can find no mentions of any financial difficulties. But then, during the trips of Jesus, these problems became obvious.

The end. Jesus was arrested and crucified. Joseph of Arimathea buried Him. It is just there Angels could and should appear again, as, in fact, they did. No matter what the situation came to, still Jesus was the last king of House of King David. He was not married; hence there would be no descendants[7]. Now, it made no sense to guard the treasures for Him; the future leader of Jewish people should be found somewhere else.

Yet it was necessary to pay the last tribute to His Royalty. The Last King of Jewish people – the real king! – had to be buried properly. You definitely agree with me, it was a serious reason to open the grave.

On Friday, Angels watched the execution and called the meeting. The situation was extra ordinal, and they had to decide what to do.

On Sunday, early in the morning, say, four o'clock, when it just began to dawn, several Angels came to the sepulchre. They moved the rock aside, came into the tomb and took off the cloths that were wrapped around Jesus' body. The King must be buried according to His title and the social rank, and His cloths had to be proper[8].

Angels treated Jesus' body with all the honours according to the royal relying ritual, put the proper cloths on Him, and re-wrapped the body. After that, they camouflaged the body as… well, actually, I do not know what they used to hide the body; and then, they took Him away to deliver The Last King to the place of His final rest.

One of the Angels stays at the open sepulchre; he is to inform someone of those coming to visit the tomb that Jesus "resurrected". They believed in something like that, His followers, didn't they? Let them go on with it. At least nobody will be looking for the King on His way to His grave, and nobody would disturb His rest.

Soon, as expected, there comes Mary Magdalene, and the story is told to her. Mary Magdalene, in her turn, accepts the story either believing it or understanding all the advantages of its existence. The story coincides with the predictions of Jesus and promises eternal glory to Him. More than that, the story supports Jesus' doctrine greatly, introducing further contribution in it, and makes the event incomparable. *The predicted miracle has happened.*

15

And here, if we choose this version, an interesting question appears: where did Angels took Jesus' body to bury? The Angels were clever people, they used to make analysis of a situation and to reckon distant consequences of the actions; plus they had almost unlimited resources. Thus they had good possibilities to take the body almost any place they chose. The only limits were the external temperature during the day and the speed of decomposition of the body, as the smell of decaying would inevitably attract undesirable attention to the carriage. And that was already the third day since Jesus' death…

The place of Jesus' new burial should have been of particular importance, otherwise, in principle, all the rituals of royal burial could be performed without removing the body from the place of the original burial. After performing the rituals, the sepulchre could be closed again and the stone would be returned to its place. It was hardly possible to expect someone being interested in robbing or opening the grave of a beggar who died on the cross or just a poor man's grave as it seemed to be.

But if we admit the supposition that The Last King was carried to His treasures… then I seem to know how to find the legendary treasures, the grave of Jesus, and the confirming the story manuscripts.

16

But what about Mary Magdalene? She, taking advantage of the general dismay and confusion, disappeared. For the journey, she used the rest of the common money left in the bag. Otherwise, how else could she escape? The disappearance of the money, as I already mentioned above, most probably caused Judas being branded as a thief.

The supposition that Mary Magdalene moved to France, which made her if not famous, than well-known there, is possible but rather unlikely. Unlikely – because in this case she would inevitably attract the attention of other disciples including Peter; but this was the situation she obviously tried to avoid. Mary Magdalene did everything to bring glory to the name of Christ, and it was not in her interests either to compromise Him or to become hunted. Apart of this, taking into consideration possibility of vengeance – no matter from whose side, by whom and for what reason it could be done – it could be dangerous for her and her coming baby.

Therefore in order to avoid any attention, Mary Magdalene had to tell that she was a widow, whose husband was killed either by Romans, or by somebody else, or died during the journey; such stories were rather typical those days and would never surprise anybody.

Angels were not looking for her either; they had never been really interested in her. They definitely did not know anything about her state meaning pregnancy. It is clear, Mary Magdalene joined the group not long before the tragic events took place; so, they paid no attention to her. Besides, Angels were rather indignant with the preaching and healing activity of Jesus; they temporized, and watched, and waited... and were not really attentive. Obviously, they missed the special relations existing between Jesus and Mary Magdalene. Angels were clever people, but they were *only* people; they made mistakes too. What's more – nobody expected such development of the events, and *such rapid* development of the events. None of the Angels knew how hard the pressure of the System could be.

Most possible, Mary Magdalene gave birth to a girl, to whom she either told or more probable did not run a risk to tell the truth about her father. She had to protect her daughter and to secure her future; that is why it was most doubtful that she told her daughter who her father really was. A person can not incur troubles caused by his/her origin not knowing it him-/herself.

Besides, if it was a boy, he might want to avenge his father, or to decide to follow His steps. He would be much more insistent in his questionings. We would probably hear about him, but a girl… After the death of Jesus the position of women in the world was changed not as quickly as He wanted to and completely in the wrong direction.

Notes

1. It is known, that to some of them Jesus said the words *"Follow me."* Obeying the order, these people followed Jesus permanently and continued His work after His death. Later, these people became the core of Christianity, and we call them now disciples or Apostles in the Orthodox tradition. Others, i.e., Judas Iscariot and Mary Magdalene, joined the group voluntarily. Later, they acted differently from the majority of the group. Not like the rest of the group, these two kept their free will and made their own choices.

2. Gospel of Mark (*14:44-45*) provides us with an interesting detail: during the arrest Judas said, "Take him and lead him away *safely;*" he tried to protect Jesus even then.

3. To the point, the fact, that Jesus in His age of 33 still wasn't married yet, does not seems to be quite natural and also can be explained by Him being a king even without kingdom. He could get married later, but He needed to marry a *proper* girl.

4. Different gospels describe the event differently (*Mathew 28:1-8; Mark 16:1-10; John 20:1-18; Luke 24:1-10*)

5. Mathew 28:2-7; Mark 16:5-6; Luke 24:4-6

6. Primarily via Joseph, I assume. He was the most informed person in the story; Angels spoke to him about marriage, about journeys, about the birth of the child, etc.

7. It is remarkable, though, that Jesus' brothers and sisters mentioned in gospels were not considered to be worth any attention. Was it because they had not been brought up properly, or because they have already had families and it would not be possible to keep the secret? Were there, maybe, some other reasons involved? Actually, it is the item for a separate research, which I plan to perform later.

8. Hence we have a perfect explanation why the shroud and the cloths covering Jesus' body under the "first" burial, were left in the cave.

Inference

We approach the end of the story. Here from, the era of Christianity begins. It took approximately two hundred years to form the basic principles and traditions of Christianity, and its development still continues. Nowadays, there are lots of different Christian confessions, and members of each of them are absolutely sure that only their vision of Christianity is right and proper. However, it is not possible to discuss questions of belief in terms of logic.

If we cast an eye over the twenty centuries that passed since the events marking the beginning of Christianity took place, we would be stricken of how many people died and were killed because of their religious views and differences in them. Tortures of first Christians, deaths caused by crusades, St. Bartholomew's Day massacre, Inquisition, men and women who were accused to be witches and sorcerers and were burnt on fires – it was of no importance if they really possessed some special powers or not; The East-West Schism[1], and Raskol[2], which took lives of people as long as in the XX century...

All that was caused by the doctrine calling to peace and tolerance; the teaching, in the name of which Jesus ended His days in such a horrible way.

By the way, as we mentioned the East-West Schism, doesn't it seem strange that it took place in general? As we know, there in Jerusalem,

Jesus preached equally to everyone, to His Jewish disciples, who are called Apostles in the Orthodox tradition, and to all the others including members of the Greek community, who later formed the Orthodox Church. The Apostles in Orthodox tradition are highly respected, but...

There still must have been a serious reason dividing the Christian movement originally led by Jesus Christ into two Christian Churches based on differences in their cultures and origin. More than that, the Churches did not simply go along each its own way, considering the way of the opponent side wrong, they became really indignant with each other. The indignation is especially remarkable from the side of representatives of the Orthodox Church.

What was the original cause of the indignation? Could it be that a very simple and obvious motivation was hidden somewhere deep in time, and the whole situation resembles the circles appearing on the surface of the water after a sudden stone fell down into the lake: the longer time has passed since the moment of the fall – the greater circles become? Let us try to find the answer to the question.

It is well-known, that the strongest and the most durable reactions of people are typically caused by something wounding personality, personal interests, and especially personal feelings. In such cases, the negative attitude lasts for years, sometimes getting even stronger with the time. So, what personal element might be involved there, 2000 years ago in ancient Jerusalem, causing the negative attitude of Greek pupils of Jesus towards the Jewish ones? And, maybe, not against all, but against one *in particular*?

Yes, I mean Peter (Simon). To be more exact, I mean that the Greek pupils of Jesus did not accept Peter's personal characteristics, meaning his merchant way of thinking, which did not correspond to the Jesus' doctrine of unselfishness and modesty. Nevertheless, this reason might be secondary corresponding to the main source of the irritation: the true Peter's feelings to Jesus, which were clearly seen from the outsider's point of view and were far from being acceptable, no matter if Peter himself did or did not understand them.

None of the pupils wanted to cast a shadow on Jesus; but it was hardly possible not to notice, not to see, and not to understand such things and relations. As I have already mentioned, people can forget the cause, but they remember the feelings. History preserved these feeling to our days, although the reason for them was hidden and forgotten long time ago.

I want you to pay attention to the following: in the countries, where Catholicism became the dominant religion, the place of women in the society is far from being equal to that of men even nowadays. Women still, though in a way[3], are considered to be submissive and meant to be used by men. The same situation, though in less extend, is being observed in the countries where the dominant religion is Lutheranism / Protestantism, which descends from Catholicism.

Let us add here the celibacy of Catholic priests: Peter hated and despised women for their sexuality, which was disgusting for him. Especially if we take into consideration that he was in love with a man and had no possibility to satisfy his passion – and probably, as I said, not knowing about it himself[4]. All Peter's unexploited sexual energy found its way out in religious fanaticism; hormonal processes in the human body can't be cancelled or simply changed by a wish of the person. At the same time, Peter's negative attitude to women remained. This attitude, apparently, survived during millennia and enslaved millions of people, women first of all.

The general attitude towards women in the Orthodox Church is much more tolerant, despite of the fact that more stringent rules are typical for the Orthodox Church in general. The same may be said about the countries where the Orthodox Church is a dominant religion: the position of women in the society in these countries is much closer to being equal to those of men.

To the point, merchant mentality of Peter was fully inherited by the Catholic Church. It was there, in the Catholic Church, the doctrine of the storehouse of merit, acquired by Jesus' sacrifice and the virtues and penances of the saints, was invented. In the Middle Ages, it resulted in selling of indulgences, i.e., promises of freedom from punishment by God, which was performed by priests and authorities of the Church.

Regarding to Peter, we have an indirect confirmation of the fact that he deliberately lied when telling about the first appearance of Jesus Christ to him after the "resurrection". If you remember, it was then (*John 21:17*), Jesus forgave Peter for his threefold denying and appointed Peter "the most important" among the disciples[5].

And here comes the explanation.

You see, even during The Last Sapper, Jesus did not pay much attention to Peter's future denial of Him. Jesus simply *mentioned* it, as if speaking of a trifle, being concentrated on the terrible future He expected, giving His last orders to the disciples, and persuading Judas to do what He meant to be necessary[6]. The disciples were shocked by the words of Jesus about the coming (Judas) betrayal, worried because of Jesus' state, and surprised by His actions when Jesus for the first time performed the Eucharist. Thus there was only one person to whom these words of Jesus really made big difference; and this person was Peter himself.

Later, after Jesus' death, Peter had guilty conscience – he *indeed* denied Jesus precisely as predicted, and maybe some other disciples were witnesses to that too. But the worst thing was that Peter did love Jesus, and *could not forgive himself* for betraying Him. *He never meant it; it was just because his instinct of self-defence predominated that moment; he was frightened so much!..* He *needed* to feel himself forgiven – and he lied about it telling the story of Jesus' resurrection and His talk to him. Jesus' forgiveness was of such importance to

Peter that he repeated the story again and again until he himself believed its truthfulness.

But then, there came the time when Jesus indeed showed Himself to Peter. It happened much later, at the very end of Peter's life. Let us recollect how it was.

According to the legend, that time Peter preached in Rome creating the Christian community and incurring anger of the authorities. To avoid the arrest, Peter left Rome at night following the advice of his pupils, who warned him about the danger. Soon after Peter left the city gates, he saw Jesus and appealed to Him with the question:

> "Quo vadis, Domine?" – Latin: "Where do you go, God?"

The response was,

> "Eo Romam iterum crucifigi," – Latin: "Going to Rome, to be crucified again," *(Acts of Peter)*

With these words, Christ rose to heaven and Peter, realizing the words as prediction of his own martyrdom, returned to Rome. Here, he was arrested, put into jail and sentenced to death by crucifixion. Not wishing to insult God being equal to Him in his death, Peter requested to be crucified his head down. Being crucified, Peter made his last homily: he told about the sacred symbolic of the Cross. The inverted cross is the symbol of Adam, whose Original Sin distorted the divine order established by God, but the upright cross is the symbol of Jesus Christ, who restored the original order; vertical part of the cross symbolises *Logos*, the word, divine in God-Man, and horizontal part symbolises the human nature in Him. Having finished these words, Peter breathes his last.

A short, depicting a conflict of the person with himself, and full of contradictions story.

But that is utter nonsense! How possibly could Peter take the words of Jesus, "Going to Rome, to be crucified again" *referring to him*, if just after he talked about *not being equated to Jesus* even in his death begging to be crucified upside down?!! No, the reasons and the motives of Peter's words and actions were absolutely different.

It is true, that his entire life Peter preached the teaching of Jesus Christ – though the way he understood it himself. It is most likely, that Peter's pupils indeed warned him against the coming arrest so as Peter left Rome. And I *do believe* that Peter really saw Jesus Christ outside the city gates, and the talk took place indeed, coming to us precisely as it was with all the details. That was the first and the only appearance of Jesus Christ to Peter.

When thinking about the talk, we can't help noticing that that moment Peter behaved himself *weird*. You see, it is only natural to ask a neighbour or a friend whom you used to see every day and with whom you used to chat, "Hi, where d'ye go, buddy?" when meeting the one in the street; but to apply *to the God* in this way when all of a sudden seeing Him?.. Who, among all believers, would act like this? No, it definitely does not seem to be appropriate.

We can find the only explanation of such words of Peter if we agree, that Peter acted as a person who was greatly shocked and confused. Strictly speaking, Peter's question was totally meaningless, "*Where do you go, God?*" as if it made any difference for Peter and especially for Jesus Christ at the moment.

Would Peter be not so much shocked, he'd probably do the same thing every believer would do leaving for the long way and facing the God – and especially when escaping in the moment of danger: *he would ask for blessing*. But at the moment of great confusion, people typically make and say some strange or stupid things, being surprised themselves when recollecting the event later. The act, when Peter asked this question, as well as the question itself, obviously belongs to this category of actions. Nevertheless, Peter asked the question and received the answer, *"Going to Rome, to be crucified again,"* the words Peter *never* should put at his own expense. That moment, Christ spoke *about Himself,* and *only* about Himself. He *had* already been crucified once, and He *would be* crucified again.

Appearance of Christ caused a great shock to Peter. When such things happen, people can't help being shocked. Then, all of a sudden, Peter recollected the old story, which he told first time soon after the "resurrection" and repeated again so many times later. He repeated it so many times, that almost convinced himself in its truthfulness. Peter recollected that *there was no story at all, nothing happened then, he invented everything himself. He lied about actions of God* even if it was done for good. Then, Peter became frightened, *he did wrong, he made the deception, which was known to God, and which he admitted himself now.* That moment, Peter became deeply upset; and he was full of repentance – and that was why he returned to Rome. He returned to be punished for what he'd done to his God.

All the time remained to his execution, Peter devotes to the excruciating thoughts. He recollects his entire life turning it in his mind over and over again – *what else did he wrong, not the way Jesus taught him?* You see, when talking to him, Jesus said not a single word of greeting or simply a good word, neither said He a word of gratitude or encouragement. Jesus Christ only *answered Peter's question;* and the meaning of the answer was negative referring to the worst event ever happened until then – the crucifixion, which meant martyrdom and death for Jesus.

The results of the speculations lead Peter into the state of horror. In fact, he distorted the teaching of Christ – and first of all, because he lied about Him. But now it is too late; it is impossible either to change or to correct anything. The foundation of Christianity is already laid, and the teaching already got its followers in different countries. If he makes the statement that it was *only now* he saw Christ and not *that time,* that he *lied* about it then, what would remain of the legend and of the teaching? And a terrible idea comes into Peter's mind: he decides to punish himself the worst way he can invent. Peter invents the concept of the inverted cross.

You see, in the vast majority of early traditions, the cross was equilateral having all the arms of equal length. Crosses on the high stalk were used by the Romans for execution of criminals, and its shape was made according to proportions of human body. Besides, it would be more difficult to escape from a cross of such proportions, i.e., from a cross standing on a high stalk, in case if somebody would try to save the criminal. In addition, this type of cross was easier to build and to install, than equilateral one. Pure practical, no sacred or hidden reasons were used to manufacture such type of crosses.

Exactly this type of cross appeared in the fevered Peter's imagination. Jesus was crucified on such cross; it was His mortuary way to Heaven. If the upright cross was the way to Heaven, the inverted cross, consequently, should be the way to hell. That was the terrible sentence given to Peter by the most pitiless judge: by himself. For his lies to God and about Him, Peter sentenced himself to eternal suffering in Hell. He requested to be crucified upside gown, with his head pointing the way his soul should go.

Before his dead, Peter tried to tell surrounding him people about his thoughts; he was trying to explain himself – as much as he dared.

He'd better remain silent! *That* was the beginning of Satanism; the way to Hell was invented. Jesus Christ was indeed crucified the second time in Rome.

I have no doubt that Jesus Christ really appeared in front of Peter, as well as He appeared in front of many other people. You see, the System, about which we have already spoken, functions in such a way, that the soul of the person, who possessed such great inner power as Jesus Christ, after the death may become, so to say, a protecting program[7, 8]. When a true believer sincerely appeals to Him – or to Her meaning saints or Goddesses – the program defends the believers from certain troubles and gives them ease and relaxation. All the rest – I mean visual appearances of the God and the saints to believers – are questions of belief, visualization, and vividness of the imagination.

As for Christianity… the building, when being built on a curved foundation, though gives protection to the people living in it, can't stand straight and runs a risk to fall into pieces. Something like that happened to Christianity; that's why we have so many different Christian confessions nowadays; and that's why they are not always friendly to each other.

There were and there are people declaring good things, but doing something quite opposite – in Christianity as well (or rather as bad) as in any other religion, as well as among not religious people. Still, when speaking of Christianity, we must admit that even now, after the 2000 years that passed since the events took place, there are fanatics willing to destroy anyone, whose points of view differ from their own with the same enthusiasm, with which the crowds of believers shouted, *"Crucify Him!"* supporting the ruling church and struggling against new ideas and the alternative points of view in a vain attempt to push it all away and to stop the progress.

Yes, there are 10 commandments, and there are records of teachings of Christ that should – and perhaps did – change the world into the better place to live in. But who is able to count how much people were killed in the name of the words *"Do not kill"*?

Happily enough, there are and there have always been people who were and are able to create new ideas and alternative views; and there were and there are other, open-minded people willing to support them. Fortunately, people are able to learn and to change their points of view – thus progress is going on.

As for the treasures, they could not be possibly inherited either by Knights Templar, or by the Church of Peter, i.e., the Roman-Catholic

Church, or by the Greek Orthodox Church. Angels – if they really existed – never supported either Jesus in His founding of Christianity or His followers. As they did not give support even to Jesus Christ Himself, who never became King Jesus, what would possibly made them to convey the treasures to the people guilty in His death, i.e., to Christians? Obviously, from the point of view of Angels, if these people never supported Jesus in His strange and superfluous ideas, maybe He would return to His normal life again, got married and gave birth to a new king, who probably would serve the people of Israel better.

That is why I'm sure: the treasures still remain in the hidden place waiting for the time to be found – perhaps together with the remains of Jesus Christ and the manuscripts telling the truth about the origin and the life of Jesus from Nazareth, The Last King of Israel.

Notes

1. The East–West Schism divided medieval Christianity into Eastern (Greek) and Western (Latin) branches, which later became known as the Eastern Orthodox Church and the Roman Catholic Church, respectively.

2. The splitting of the Russian Orthodox Church into an official church and the Old Believers movement, 1666–1667.

3. Meaning lower salary, less number of women in certain professions and in leading positions in society, etc.

4. Here, I would like to underline: I do not blame Peter for being the person he was. I describe the situation without judging, giving neither pros nor contras. Besides, people do not choose their individual features and sexual attitudes, they just have them.

5. It can be also mentioned in this connection, that the Orthodox Church recognizes Saint Peter's leading role in the early church,

especially in the very early days at Jerusalem, but does not consider him to have any "princely" role over other Apostles.

6. Although, who knows what would happen to the world if it was not done then? What would our world look like today? Most probably, all those visions, haunting Jesus and pushing Him to the crucifixion, became true.

7. Here, I deliberately simplify the things. To receive the detailed explanations is necessary to learn the Theory of the Alternative Understanding of the World, and those interested in it are welcome to apply to the Danish Academy of Human and Nature. The lectured and the seminars may be provided.

8. Apart of the described situation, as life shows us, belief of immense mass of people make "protecting programs" out of ordinary people as, e.g., Peter (Simon), disciples, and other saints.

Bibliography

1. Н.В. Пулло. Книга в трех словах. Available in Russian, lectures and seminars on the item may be provided. http://proza.ru/texts/2006/12/26-123.html

2. Libby Fairhurst. Jesus walked on ice, says study led by FSU scientist. Florida State University FSU.Com http://www.fsu.com/pages/2006/04/04/WalkedOnIce.html

3. Marie-Louise von Franz. Eventyrfortolkning. På dansk ved Hanne Møller (Kbh.): Gyldendal, 1989

4. В.И.Вернадский. Несколько слов о ноосфере. http://vernadsky.lib.ru/e-texts/archive/noos.html

5. Н.В. Пулло. Вторая ступень. Available in Russian, lectures and seminars on the item may be provided.

6. Посмертные вещания преподобного Нила Мироточивого Афонского. Издание Сретенского монастыря, 2003.

7. Ольга Максимова. Жизнь и смерть Иуды Искариота. Журнал «Наука и религия». «НиР» 2/2008 ONLINE

8. http://www.n-i-r.ru/nir2.php?id_stat=255

9. Александр Чижевский. Солнечные пятна и психозы (Гелиопсихология) http://psyfactor.org/gelio2.htm

General Reading

1. Acts of Peter, http://wesley.nnu.edu/biblical_studies/noncanon/acts/actpete.htm

2. Bilde, Per . Gnosticism, Jewish Apocalypticism and Early Christianity. i: In the Last Days, Århus 1994, xx.

3. Bilde, Per. En religion bliver til: en undersøgelse af kristendommens forudsætninger og tilblivelse indtil år 110. - Frederiksberg : Anis, 2002

4. Catholic Encyclopedia, The. http://www.newadvent.org/cathen/index.html

5. Gospel According to Mary Magdalene, The . http://www.gnosis.org/library/marygosp.htm

6. Gospel of Judas, The. http://209.85.135.104/search?q=cache:_Cp8w0ij9lUJ: www.nationalgeographic.com/lostgospel/_pdf/GospelofJudas. pdf+the+gospel+of+judas+text&hl=en&ct=clnk&cd= 3&gl=us&client=firefox-a

7. Gospel of Peter, The. http://www.earlychristianwritings.com/text/gospelpeter-brown.html

8. Gospel of Thomas. http://www.gnosis.org/naghamm/gosthom.html

9. Holly Bible, The . 21st Century King James Version. http://www.biblegateway.com/versions/?action=getVersionInfo&vid=48

10. Infancy Gospel of Thomas, The. http://www.gnosis.org/library/inftoma.htm

11. Wolf Messing, an enigmatic 'psychic entertainer' whom Sathya Sai Baba claims to have encountered. http://saibaba-invigilator.blogspot.com/2009/07/wolf-messing-enigmatic-psychic.htm

12. Бехтерев, В.М.. Внушение и его роль в общественной жизни. http://psyfactor.org/lib/behterev.htm

13. Библия. Синодальный перевод. http://days.pravoslavie.ru/Bible/Index.htm

14. Бурлешин, Михаил . Тайная жена Иисуса. Газета «Тайная власть», 5/2005 http://www.privatelife.ru/2005/tv05/n5/2.html

15. Вольф Мессинг. http://messing.ho.com.ua/pub/

16. Всемирная история. http://enc.mail.ru/encycl.html?encycl_id=whist

17. Всемирный биографический энциклопедический словарь. http://enc.mail.ru/encycl.html?encycl_id=biog

18. Гелиопсихология (Солнечный фактор в нашей жизни). http://psyfactor.org/gelio.htm

19. Евангелие детства. (Евангелие от Фомы). http://www.vehi.net/apokrify/detstva.html

20. Евангелие от Марии. http://www.sacrum.ru/Christ/maria.htm

21. Евангелие от Петра. http://www.biblicalstudies.ru/Lib/NTApok/EPetr.html

22. Евангелие от Фомы. Библиотека «Вехи». http://www.vehi.net/apokrify/foma.html

23. Протоиерей Владимир Башкиров, магистр богословия. Праздник Петра и Павла. Минские духовные школы. http://minds.by/article/108.html

24. Российский энциклопедический словарь. http://enc.mail.ru/encycl.html?encycl_id=res

25. Солнце: подтверждаются худшие прогнозы. Обозреватель. http://www.obozrevatel.com/news/2006/3/10/96147.htm

26. Черкасская, Анна. Вольф Мессинг / Wolf Messing. Луна и гроши http://www.peoples.ru/state/divinators/messing/

27. Чижевский А.Л. Земное эхо солнечных бурь. http://readall.ru/lib_page_readall_106448.html

28. Чижевский А.Л. Космический пульс жизни. http://www.ionization.ru/issue/iss63.htm

29. Чижевский, Александр. Солнечные пятна и психозы (Гелиопсихология) http://psyfactor.org/gelio2.htm

30. Чижевский, Александр. Физические факторы исторического процесса. http://astrologic.ru/library/chizhevsky/index.htm

31. Энциклопедический словарь Брокгауза и Евфрона. http://enc.mail.ru/encycl.html?encycl_id=brok

32. Энциклопедия «Мифы народов мира». http://enc.mail.ru/encycl.html?encycl_id=mif

33. Энциклопедия «Народы и религии мира». http://enc.mail.ru/encycl.html?encycl_id=narod

THE DANISH ACADEMY
OF PEOPLE AND NATURE

The DACPN provides scientific research within traditional and non-traditional studies of people and nature and gives a platform to scientists for discussions and free exchange of opinions within the items of studies of the DACPH aiming further development of science.

The DACPN proposes challenging education on the courses of the Academy in the item of own research, the Theory of Alternative Understanding of the World, as well as on relative subjects. The graduates will receive a certificate or a diploma correspondingly to the fulfilled program.

The DACPN proposes innovative technologies, materials, and know-how to protect nature and human beings against industrial pollution and to restore the ecology. The DACPN provides monitoring of the state of polluted zones and territories anomalous including. The suggestion for their normalization will be proposed in the report if possible. The research includes studying paranormal phenomena.

The DACPN works in cooperation with scientific institutions and public organizations of several countries international including. In this connection, institutions, companies and organizations, including universities and NGOs as well as professionally interested individuals, who would be of relevance for the research of the Academy, are invited to contact the DACPN.

The DACPN gratefully accepts donations and sponsorship from individuals and organizations. The funds will be directed to the development of the Academy. The name of the sponsor will be shown on the website of the DACPN at his request.

Account numbers of the Academy:

Account, USD: 3282168677
IBAN: DK5630003282168677
S.W.I.F.T. DABADKKK

EURO: 3282168669
IBAN: DK7830003282168669
S.W.I.F.T. DABADKKK

Contact information:
Danish Academy of People and Nature
Runddyssen 186, DK-9230 Svenstrup J, Denmark
E-mail: dacpn@dacpn www.dacpn.dk